"This book is difficult to read—as any ho... must be. But it is rich and indispensable to any on this hard journey or walking with another who is. Here we witness a father's crushed heart desperately reaching for grace and truth. It is a story told with searing honesty, genuine doubt, and sustaining faith. Mel is the guide we need for the journey we do not want."

Scott Arbeiter, president of World Relief

"When the unthinkable happens to those you love most, you cope, you drag your legs out of bed in the morning, you walk as in a stupor, you move one foot in front of the other, and you limp like Jacob. The limp never goes away. This book is about the horrific, tragic death of Eva, the author's daughter, and the book is painful to read. Mel and Ingrid will limp until they die, but their limping is somehow a grace of memory that painfully reminds them of Eva. In their limping they remember Eva, they talk to Eva, they talk about Eva, they wonder and they wander, they see Eva and places she liked and they liked together. But every step, no matter how painful, is a limp with her at their side. Mel Lawrenz has been a friend for years, but I entered into his inner world in this book. Many of us are limping with Mel. At times I had to put this book down, but along the way I acquired a limp."

Scot McKnight, professor of New Testament at Northern Seminary

"Mel Lawrenz has, by some alchemy of grace and daring, taken the harrowing pain of losing his beloved daughter and turned it into healing balm. *A Chronicle of Grief* deserves to stand alongside C. S. Lewis's *A Grief Observed*, Gerald Sittser's *A Grace Disguised*, and Nicholas Wolterstorff's *Lament for a Son* as an experience of rawest sorrow transmuted into a testament of deepest hope. Profoundly moving and profoundly life giving."

Mark Buchanan, author of *David: Rise* and *God Speed: Walking as a Spiritual Practice*

"Mel Lawrenz has written lucidly and beautifully about the death of his beloved adult daughter. His transparent description of the overwhelming grief he experienced and the solace he found in the Lord and the community of faith is moving, instructive, and most helpful. Highly recommended."

Jill Briscoe, founding editor of *Just Between Us*, teacher on Telling the Truth

"Within the pages of *A Chronicle of Grief*, Mel Lawrenz bares his heart broken with grief, yet his story is sprinkled with hope. As I write we are in the middle of the COVID-19 pandemic, which is ripping so many from the arms of their loved ones. When he wrote this book, the author would have had no inkling of what was to come. So much death . . . so much loss . . . so much trauma . . . so much grief . . . for so many individuals and families. *A Chronicle of Grief* could not be more timely."

Heather Davediuk Gingrich, professor of counseling at Denver Seminary, author of *Restoring the Shattered Self*

MEL LAWRENZ

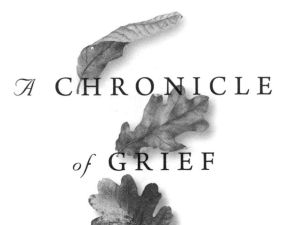

A CHRONICLE

of GRIEF

Finding Life After Traumatic Loss

ivp

An imprint of InterVarsity Press
Downers Grove, Illinois

InterVarsity Press
P.O. Box 1400, Downers Grove, IL 60515-1426
ivpress.com
email@ivpress.com

InterVarsity Press® is the book-publishing division of InterVarsity Christian Fellowship/USA®, a
movement of students and faculty active on campus at hundreds of universities, colleges, and schools of
nursing in the United States of America, and a member movement of the International Fellowship of
Evangelical Students. For information about local and regional activities, visit intervarsity.org.

All Scripture quotations, unless otherwise indicated, are taken from The Holy Bible, New International
Version®, NIV®. Copyright © 1973, 1978, 1984, 2011 by Biblica, Inc.™ Used by permission of Zondervan.
All rights reserved worldwide. www.zondervan.com. The "NIV" and "New International Version" are
trademarks registered in the United States Patent and Trademark Office by Biblica, Inc.™

While any stories in this book are true, some names and identifying information may have been
changed to protect the privacy of individuals.

Photo of Eva Lawrenz used courtesy of the author
Cover design and image composite: David Fassett
Interior design: Daniel van Loon
Images: autumn oak leaf: © assalve / E+ / Getty Images
　　　blue sky: © John O'neill / EyeEm / Getty Images
　　　green oak leaves: © Creativ Studio Heinemann / Getty Images
　　　leaf skeleton: © Kenny Williamson / Moment Collection / Getty Images
　　　watercolor of a leaf: © cat_arch_angel / iStock / Getty Images Plus

ISBN 978-0-8308-3760-1 (print)
ISBN 978-0-8308-3922-3 (digital)

Printed in the United States of America ∞

InterVarsity Press is committed to ecological stewardship and to the conservation of natural resources
in all our operations. This book was printed using sustainably sourced paper.

Library of Congress Cataloging-in-Publication Data

A catalog record for this book is available from the Library of Congress.

P	25	24	23	22	21	20	19	18	17	16	15	14	13	12	11	10	9	8	7	6	5	4	3	2	1
Y	37	36	35	34	33	32	31	30	29	28	27	26	25	24	23	22	21	20							

*This book is dedicated
to those who have suffered
devastating loss and are
hoping to survive—and
something more.*

CONTENTS

1

TRAUMA

$\mathcal{I}$ was in an unpleasant discussion at work when my cell phone sounded that simple and unobtrusive "ding" that meant a text message had arrived. A few minutes later I slipped the phone out of my pocket and read: "Eva not breathing. Pray."

What I was looking at made no sense. I stared at the screen. My brain locked up. I felt a wave of dread wash over my body. And then adrenaline. I ducked into an empty room and used my phone to call my wife and learned that my thirty-year-old daughter was in an ambulance being whisked away to a hospital, paramedics applying resuscitation.

This is a survival story.

The worst thing that happened in my early life was the death of my father when I was four. Then, when I was a father of a high school age son who was in a near-fatal auto accident—that was the worst.

But then came the *unthinkable* worst, on that early June day our beautiful daughter collapsed and died, and all the tortures that followed. Life became even more complicated in the months that followed when I had a serious accident, and then my mother died. But the worst, the worst of the worst, was losing our daughter. The fourteen-month window when all this happened seemed too much to bear.

My first thought on that June day was that we had entered a harsh new reality. I had no say in this reality. The ground had dropped away directly in front of where I was standing, and our daughter had disappeared.

How can this be? What do we do now? What will happen to us?

Since that time I constantly think about the people around me who have gone through searing loss. For some, the death of a loved one; for others, divorce, being betrayed, having a dreadful disease, losing a career, being assaulted or abused, or any other experience that is overwhelming. There is so much we have to survive, and hopefully do better than just survive. How we need other people who care. How we need to be able to access our faith in God, however that works out.

I look around now and I see people everywhere who are suffering some kind of excruciating loss, and they are having a hard time figuring out what to do.

Facing traumatic loss is about keeping our sanity and taking care of those who depend on us, all the while deciding how we are going to face this new unwelcome reality. I learned at so many points that I had to look straight at the loss or I could not find comfort. On the other hand, surviving also meant using distractions and diversions in order to interrupt ascending panic, especially in those early days. We do what we have to do. It's not wrong if we have to leave the lights or television on in order to sleep. It's okay to interrupt obsessive thoughts. It's important to be honest with people who want to know how we are doing.

To unload the burden, I wrote a few paragraphs each month and sent them to friends or posted them on social media. I was surprised that so many people said this writing was helpful to them. Some said it helped them know they are normal in their own reactions to a terrible loss. Others found practical help. And still others just wanted to know there is hope. No one survives on their own.

In that first year I found that writing something, about once a month, and sharing it with others somewhat lessened the weight that was smashing me into the ground. I wrote just to get some of the pain off my chest. This was not an exercise in self-reflection or the discipline of journaling. It was about survival. Taking the edge off the pain. Crying out. Proclaiming love through confessing devastation. A search for meaning, I suppose.

A lot of people responded to me and my family by suffering with us, which is, of course, the literal meaning of *sympathy*. This is the height of compassion, when someone goes beyond feeling sorry, in some mysterious way suffering *with* us.

I kept thinking about all the people slain by the pain of traumatic loss who may not know what to do to get through the most difficult days. Who do not find many sympathetic voices around them or who feel some external necessity to feel or behave a certain way. When the dam broke one day two years later and I started writing this book, I was thinking about all of us who know that life goes on but don't understand how when life itself seems cut off.

I hope there is something here to help if you or a loved one are plunged into survival mode. The chapters that follow include the experiences and some epiphanies that happened in the first three years after our loss—particularly the first twelve months. I recognize that three years into our experience is not a long way, and that we will know so much more five years and ten years from now. But I wanted to write while these experiences were fresh in my mind.

Traumatic loss has a way of slowing time down. Now, three years later, time moves along at a more or less normal pace. But six months after our loss, each week felt like a month. In the early weeks some days felt like they would drag on forever. In the first days time seemed suspended.

For context, here is just a bit about me and my family. Ingrid and I were married when we were quite young, but it was twelve years before we had our first child, Eva. Our son, Christopher, came along two years later. Ingrid and I both experienced hardship and loss as kids, and so when she became a social worker and a professional counselor and I, a pastor, we felt fairly prepared to deal with the core issues of struggles in life. We both have loved doing our work, though helping people with major life problems is difficult when our own family faces one personal challenge after another. We dealt with health issues Ingrid had and a near-fatal auto accident Christopher came through, but when Eva died we came to a crossroads. Would we survive or not?

I had cowritten two books on grief and trauma years ago, and I suppose that helped us when we had to face the unspeakable loss of our beautiful daughter. But teaching about traumatic loss is one thing, getting slain in a day of trauma, another.

Traumatic loss is a technical term. Roughly speaking, it means experiencing something that is unexpected, jarring, and devastating, which causes injury with long-term effects. Soldiers experience trauma. If our house burns to the ground, we might experience trauma. Someone who is mugged or raped or kidnapped certainly has gone through trauma. People react differently to traumatic events. When, in an ordinary day, we have breakfast with a family member and that evening their body is at the morgue, we have gone through trauma. Our lives are fundamentally changed when we go through trauma, and some people would say they have never recovered. But it is possible to survive. To go on living. The word itself, *survive*, means to continue to live or exist, especially in spite of hardship or danger.

This book could be difficult reading. In the months that followed our daughter's death, I knew I had to be brutally honest. That to receive full comfort, I had to gaze straight ahead at the pain. I had a strong desire to find the solid ground of faith in God beneath my feet, but I knew that voicing mindless spiritual clichés would be like blowing bubbles. Platitudes fall flat. There are things we can do to survive, and more. We need to find those ways.

So, here it is.

2

HORRIFIC

Survival, in those early days and weeks, was primal and physical. We did what we needed to do to get through each day and each hour of each day.

Every minute of the three-hour drive from Brookfield, Wisconsin, to the hospital in Sturgeon Bay was torture. I tried to shut my brain off and step out of time and just keep the car on the road. It was just me and the sound of tires on the road.

When I rushed out of the house I knew that Eva was in an ambulance two hundred miles away being driven to a hospital while emergency workers tried to revive her. My wife, Ingrid, was with her. She had collapsed at about noon in the house in Door County where she and my wife had been visiting Ingrid's sister for a week. She had been ill for a few days. In recent years Eva had developed complicated autoimmune medical issues that had put her into a weakened medical condition. Before those years she had been an extraordinarily bright and lively young woman. Engaging and inspiring. A blonde beauty and a curious intellectual. She brought exuberance into any room she was in. But the illness had dulled her in recent years. It sapped her energy and made her withdrawn.

We had sought every diagnostic and treatment plan available. Many specialists. Test after test. Attempted treatments. But her health was still poor. Not terminal, except that a simple infection could race through her body. The next thing we knew, she was in an ambulance, unconscious and unresponsive.

By the time I got to the hospital after 150 miles of driving, she was gone. They could not revive her. My wife and I entered the darkened, silent room in the emergency wing where the medical examiner drew back the sheet covering her head.

This can't be.

At that moment I knew we had entered a different world with a harsh new reality. I knew that one cold, bare task was before us or else we would be destroyed: to accept this reality.

It is an absolute reality. Every other hardship and challenge I had faced in life before—and there were many—held at least the slight possibility of a solution. But death is an absolute dividing line. Despite the reality of heaven and future redemption, at the moment a loved one breathes their last breath, a divide opens up like the ground splitting between us. Some people are stunned into numbness, and none of it seems real. Not me. I could see it all in its starkness. No breath, no movement, no sound.

Done. Real. Irreversible.

A harsh new reality. A division. A frightening void. Absolute sentence.

No fixing. No negotiating. No delay.

Gone.

An hour later I called my eighty-six-year-old mother and choked out words I found incomprehensible to be saying, "Mom . . . Eva died today." After I explained a bit, her first words, shaky and tentative, were, "What are we going to do?" In the face of danger our instincts drive us to action. We feel we must *do* something. Our instincts are to try to solve the crisis which is more massive than we could have imagined. But there is nothing to do. At least, nothing that will make those lungs expand and eyes open.

Within minutes we are, of course, forced to act. We have to answer the many questions of the medical examiner, to tell the funeral home director what we want to be done with transporting the body, to contact family and friends. We had to drive back home the long three hours where our son waited. He was overwhelmed with fear and anxiety. Later that night I had to answer a battery of questions on the phone from the organ donation people. Was I actually answering unending health-history questions on this day?

Please, let it stop.

The three of us slept on furniture in our living room that night, lights on, television on in the background, which was better than dreadful silence. I felt a chill in the house.

The next day pastors came to the house. One started heading back from Wyoming to get back in time to lead the music at the funeral. Action required. We had to pick a date, select songs, write an obituary. Ingrid jumped into it, and all of her instincts were right.

The quiet hours were the hardest, when we were alone with our thoughts. When my mind approached the harsh reality, I tried to face it, but fear and panic surged through my body without warning. *What is going to happen? What are we going to do? What has actually happened here? How can it be possible that we are not able to hug her and comfort her as we did for the years she was ill? How can everything so abruptly and severely end?*

The whole thing seemed absurd. Evil and absurd.

I had a sense of dread and foreboding. It was like a grizzly bear had descended on our family camp and dragged one member away, and the same monster was still afoot and anyone else in the family could get dragged away at any moment. The dread was unexpected and overwhelming. Death seemed like a power in itself. A wicked, gory monster. This should not have happened. Thirty years old is too young. *Who will be next?*

The day after, I dragged Eva's mattress out of her bedroom and down the stairs: thump, thump, thump. Then wrestled it through the door and out to the road where, just a few minutes later, the trash collectors arrived and threw it in their truck. I watched. I felt a hatred for that bed. Eva's autoimmune disease had caused her to spend far too many days in that bed. It had collapsed in the middle. It had to go—immediately. When the trash collectors drove away I felt just a little bit cleansed. It was necessary to do more than stare at the void. I had to step into it. But it was a battle. A battle with open air.

Her bedroom now contradicted the harsh new reality. A half-drunk can of soda. A trash can with food wrappers.

Clothes scattered here and there. A book lying open. The smell of her perfume in the air. These were signs of life. *So, how can she not be alive? Is this just a nightmare? How can everything change in a day?* I gathered the trash and put away the clothes and stopped every few minutes to force my lungs to breathe. At a certain point I felt overwhelmed and left the room, debating in my mind whether or not to shut the door. Do we look into the hole, or wall it off? The answer was different every day.

In those early days surviving meant getting through not just every day but every hour and every minute of every hour.

That meant cutting off escalating panic. I talked to a couple of friends who are mental health professionals about whether it is okay to use any mental trick to shut down spiraling fear. This fear was a monster. Yes, of course that's okay, they told me. In those early days and weeks that was not avoiding grieving. There would be months of grieving ahead. This was surviving. It felt good to hear that everything we were going through was normal.

So I watched cable news in order to stay present-focused, feeling embarrassed that I had to resort to something so undignified, but it helped a little. It was important, in the face of the harsh new reality, to focus on other realities of life—the big, broad world where there were dramatic things happening—most of it bad, some of it good—but it was real. It was now.

We are alive. We need to get through this. We need each other.

Sometimes the panic would subside only if I stared at different physical objects in the room. *That table is real. This chair I'm sitting in is springy. My feet are in contact with the ground. I'll count the panels in the ceiling. There, good, I can breathe again.*

We just do what we have to do. Pacing could take the edge off. Sometimes calling out Eva's name and telling her we loved her—over and over again, with sobbing—was painful, but it was the right thing to do. Ingrid and I loved her from the moment she was conceived. We had waited more than ten years for that to happen. There is no way we would allow death to stop us from loving her now. I would look up and shout out "we love you," and I knew it mattered.

Does all this seem like a family who has lost their faith? What about heaven? What about the assurance that Eva had a place in that great mystery that is the presence of God? I didn't worry then that my reactions contradicted my faith, and I do not worry about it now. Just look at the honesty of the psalms. God allows us to weep and to shout. These are the surest sign of love, God's greatest gift.

Have mercy on me, LORD, for I am faint;
heal me, LORD, for my bones are in agony.
  My soul is in deep anguish.
How long, LORD, how long? . . .

I am worn out from my groaning.
All night long I flood my bed with weeping
  and drench my couch with tears.
My eyes grow weak with sorrow. (Psalm 6:2-3, 6-7)

To fully feel the stabbing pain of loss is not a lack of faith. It is the affirmation of deep love when it is cruelly interrupted.

The faith dimension of our loss would be worked out in many ways in the months that followed. We would gain the assurances that faith in God offers—along with the pain. It is not either-or. Crying out to God in lament is no less an act of worship than praising God.

Right from the start I knew that if we did not honestly admit the horror of the harsh reality of the loss of our daughter, we would delay the blessings of reassurance and faith.

Faith begins with poverty.

3

GONE

We all experience loss and grief differently. For some, the worst thing that has happened to them is getting fired from a favorite job. For others, it is going through a divorce, being sexually assaulted, being in active combat, getting a dire medical diagnosis. Any such experience may require us to adopt survival skills while we try to get through the immediate loss and then the journey that follows.

When someone very close to us dies, we find ourselves staring at this stark reality: our loved one is gone. Just gone. And there is no bringing them back. That final breath is final. We can't call another medical specialist. We can't have a final conversation because the last one we had was the last one we will ever have, and we can't choose to have it in a different place or on a different topic. We know that now the major work of our life is going to be to accept this new harsh reality. We simply have no choice.

We fall back on our faith, if we have faith, and maybe in those early days we have some comfort, but maybe we cannot access that comfort just yet. We are staring at the edge of the cliff, eyes darting back and forth to find our loved one who was standing there just a minute ago. But she is gone. And we keep wondering how that could possibly be.

We want to talk to our loved one. Even if there is no response. A pressure inside builds; we just have to get it out.

Yet, even when someone is gone, our relationship is not nullified. The meaningful connection between us endures even if the ability to interact is gone.

Eva was our sweet daughter, and I so wanted to talk to her. And I did, calling out to her and writing directly to her. I wanted to talk to other people about her (not to brag, which she would not have approved of) but to share the joy she brought to me and Ingrid and Christopher, my sister and Ingrid's sister, and so many others.

About two weeks after Eva left us, I needed to make a call and looked at the "Favorites" list on my cell phone. There was her name, just below my wife's and just above Christopher's. EVA LAWRENZ. As I stared at her name a stark realization overwhelmed me: if I pushed that button, absolutely no one would answer. There was no one on the other end. And there never would be ever again. I sobbed and wailed.

How can that be? I thought. *I can't call you now. But I can speak to you. And I will. I will speak and write about the things you and I talked about.*

This pulls your mind in two opposite directions. You are facing the harsh reality that your loved one is gone, but you know it just cannot be that all the love, all the joy, all the personal knowing, could disappear into thin air.

Fourteen days after Eva died it was Father's Day. That was painful. Ingrid got pregnant eleven years after we were married. We were not at all sure we'd have any kids.

In my mind I spoke to Eva about how blessed I felt to be her father. For Father's Day I wrote her a note.

I don't want to brag about you, which you would not have approved of. I want to shout out about the joy you brought to me and Mom and Christopher and so many others.

I was so blessed to be your father, and still to be your father. And so blessed to see how Mom loved you from the moment you were born until the moment you died. You kept us hopping, you precocious little squirt. You were interested in everything, especially the creative . . .

I had a hard time keeping up with your understanding of literature when you were in college. Your drawings and paintings were amazing. I see in them beauty and playfulness, but also an honest dealing with and acceptance of mortality. Did you know even then that you would not have a long life? We'll never know. There are so many mysteries. So many unanswered questions. I have to trust that our days are numbered. So many of your days were truly wonderful. I am so sorry you have been so ill for the past few years. I'm glad you said you felt safe and loved in our home and family.

I knew that people would recall to us your beauty and intelligence and curiosity and liveliness and creativity. What amazed me, however, is hearing from your friends about the depth of your character. How you influenced them. How they trusted you. How you were always intensely present with anyone you talked to. How you wanted to go deep. How you were courageously honest. How you tried so hard to help others.

How you made us laugh. How you'd show kindness to total strangers.

Eva kept me honest. No spiritual game-playing. No clichés. No self-righteousness. She told me what people needed to know, and that helped me with my sermons and my books. And when I bought a sport coat or shoes that weren't wise fashion choices, one shake of her head, a quizzical look from her, a "Dad, no," and it was back to the store.

On that Father's Day, and two weeks earlier at the memorial service, I was captivated by one main thought: the person Eva was is exactly what the world needs. She expressed beauty in the face of ugliness, depth instead of superficiality, honesty instead of deception. Ingrid and Chris and I and relatives and friends felt her loss, but I also sensed a loss in the world. A loss of goodness and truth and beauty. So needed. So rare. I wrote to her that I would try, as much as I could, to talk to people about how we all need to do better, with God's help. That life is too short to play games. That we need to be selfless and completely respectful of others.

And I wondered, *Why is this not obvious to all of us all the time? Why does it take death to open our eyes to life?*

Whereas I wrote out what was going on in me, Ingrid took her time with every conversation every compassionate friend offered. Friends were wise to just let her tell the story and tell it again. Christopher chose to give tribute to his best friend and sister by posting online his favorite pictures of the two of them—ones with beaming smiles—and by telling others how Eva was an inspiration to him and how he felt his words fell far short of the honor he wanted to express. Two weeks in he wrote, "God Bless Eva Lawrenz for her beauty, purity, and intelligence that has influenced me and others and blessed our world. May she never be forgotten but loved in our hearts."

How grateful we were for the many people who came to the funeral. When our pastor friends sat down with us to plan it, Ingrid's instincts led the way. She knew what songs to pick, what readings, and we shared in picking the participants. It all fell into place. There would be one service at our home church and then another two days later in Door County, where extended family could come. That is where the cemetery of our ancestors is located. As we talked about how the week would unfold, Christopher asked me, "How are we going to do this, Dad?" I told him I didn't know, but that we would be together. Right close together. We would get through it together.

On the day of the memorial service, getting dressed had a surreal feeling to it. Like putting on armor for some kind of battle. Tying my shoes seemed like a significant act of faith. I wanted to march ahead, get it over. How would we face the people? Stand in front of the photo boards? Read the cards on the flowers? Hear the music, hear the words?

Friends came from near and far and bore us up with words and songs and prayers. Friends and colleagues and Eva's friends came. We lived in the reality of *together*. We made it through because of *together*. I was awed by the power of *together*. As we sat in the chapel in the front row, in that room where we worshiped for decades, where our kids played piano at recitals, where Eva and Chris were baptized, where I had given sermons for decades and officiated at weddings and funerals, we watched an unfolding progression of dignity. It felt like stinging antiseptic and soothing salve on wounds at the same time.

Ingrid and had decided from the start that neither of us would speak at the funeral. We did not need that pressure. As we were getting dressed to go, she said to me, "You know, you can still change your mind about saying something." I said no. She replied, "Well, if the Holy Spirit prompts you . . ." I said, "I don't care if the Holy Spirit prompts, I'm not speaking."

But in the closing moments of the service I was feeling something I was not expecting at all: challenge and conviction. Just before the closing benediction, on impulse I stood and stepped toward a microphone and choked out some words. I said that I was surprised that I was feeling overwhelmingly challenged. That if this young woman could choose truthfulness over dishonesty, depth over superficiality, beauty over the ugliness in our world, why can't we? We can do better. We must do better.

Three days later at the cemetery, with a dozen good friends and family standing around on a sunny June day, Ingrid passed out individual roses from the spray on top of the casket, and Christopher took his ring that featured a small cross on it—a ring that he associated with his own walk of survival in life—and placed it on top of the casket before it was lowered into the ground. We went to our cars. We all drove to Ingrid's sister's house, where casseroles and desserts and coffee were waiting, and we experienced again the miracle of *together*.

Months down the road I knew I was facing an important issue: Would this severe separation cause me to want to separate from people or drive me to value and seek connection? I knew that in those early frightening weeks it was our connection with friends and family that got us through. We soaked up every bit of grace and love and compassion that came our way. Every card, every meal, every conversation was a lifeline. But inevitably, after a few months, our loss was old news to most people. We could see it in people's faces. It was not that they didn't care. But the pain they felt for us had subsided, and ours was still ever-present. Thank God for the handful of friends who continued to feel strongly for us and for those who had gone through a similar loss who knew better than us that the pathway is long. They keep talking to us with a knowing look.

Grieving so often pulls us in conflicting directions. We want to be left alone, but we don't want to be alone. We want to be in the company of good people, but we have a lower tolerance for the stress that can come from being around people. One moment quiet is calming, and the next moment unbearable. We want people to ask about our loss, but not if they say something insensitive.

It is not a surprise that most people are afraid of saying the wrong thing, and not surprising they avoid saying anything at all. But this is a mistake. Somehow we think that if we ask someone about their loss that we are creating pain. This is hardly ever the case. It is far, far more painful when people ignore our loss or move on after a season rather than giving us the option of talking about it. People who are in pain always can choose to answer briefly or to say they don't want to talk about it, but they will not have that option if, after a season, people suddenly seem to forget that we are walking, bleeding.

Our connection with other people is one of the most important treasures of life. We all make choices about this. We are created to have connections, though sometimes it is hard to develop good friendships or get to know our neighbors or find a church where we fit. Illness may cause us to withdraw. Hurtful experiences may turn us into turtles drawn up into our protective shells. We may isolate ourselves because we don't want to have to give anything to anybody. But that is a kind of self-imprisonment. It will cut us off from grace. If we don't ever give, we will have a hard time receiving.

One of the greatest barriers to recovering from a heart-rending loss, ironically, is the fear of recovering. This happens at so many levels. If I find happy moments again, it feels like an insult to my daughter. If I invest in relationships, am I setting myself up for disappointment when the next person is gone in one way or another? If I make it through this, will people have all the same expectations they used to have of me? I feel permanently diminished, yet stronger—which is it?

Surviving traumatic loss is like being forced to move to a new country even though we've not physically moved an inch.

My letter to Eva on Father's Day closed with this:

> We are in a house of mourning now. We are looking for solace, and we are finding it in our faith in the character of God. There is no way that a person as lovely and good as you would ever have graced this world unless the God of all creation, who chose to create you, is the highest good and the greatest beauty. I know you are in the hands of the Father whose love for you is magnified many times more than even my love for you. And so we trust, and then we cry, and then we trust again. We love you.

4

PLODDING

William Carey went to India in 1793 in order to bring the life-saving power of the good news of Jesus Christ. It was odd, to say the least, for an Englishman who was a shoemaker, to believe he should do this audacious thing, but he felt compelled. When skeptical family members asked what qualifications he had to go to India, Carey admitted that he was not a physician, not a statesman, not an engineer. He said of himself, "I can plod."[1]

The suffering he and his wife endured would require exactly that trait, especially when a warehouse fire destroyed all his work—grammars and Bible translations, paper imported from England, dictionaries, deeds. It happened seventeen years after he began his work in India. Seventeen years of work up in flames in a single night. No hard-drive backups. No photocopies.

But Carey did not return to England. He began the same work over again. He said it went a little faster the second time. He could plod.

I used this historical story in a sermon I gave years ago, and it is the idea that people have quoted back to me more than anything else I have ever taught. It is something people hang onto, a truth that helps them survive.

I have heard it from so many people over the years, those for whom the worst is a death, a disease, a divorce, or just a sense of confusion or lostness or deflation. Most of us, unless we are absolutely paralyzed, can plod. Because plodding means simply putting one foot in front of the other. It is not just taking one day at a time but one hour at a time. Mentally and emotionally and spiritually and even physically, we trudge along. Unless we are completely derailed, we can take one step after another. We don't look at the horizon. We just look at the ground a few steps in front of that next step we take. Each step is a gift from God and an offering to God.

The early weeks were clearly the hardest. Quite different in our experience than a year later.

One month in we did each day whatever we could to make it through the day. We looked at the day ahead and made a plan. The goal was to just get through the day. Do what needs to be done, allow for times of weeping and some pacing, staying close together, letting the awful truth of Eva's absence sink in as real, receive kind well-wishes and practical help of good-hearted friends and acquaintances, tell them about Eva, watch a movie at night, go to sleep with a few lights on and the TV on in the background.

Some of the best words we heard from our friends and acquaintances at the start were, "I have no words." That showed more understanding than lots of words. *Yes! They get it! They feel it. At least some of it.* When someone said "I have no words," I knew that they knew that our loss was so enormous that they could not comprehend it. By not *getting it* they were *getting it*, in part.

One of the most comforting comments was, "I'm thinking about you today." When people said that, they were giving a great gift. They were taking a bit of their mental energy and space to hold us in their minds on a given day. It is wonderful to be remembered. So simple, so powerful. It is frightening to think I will be forgotten. In reality most people will forget about our loss a few weeks or months down the line. They may even assume we've gotten over it because they have.

When we are in the middle of the worst, we may get words of sympathy from friends and family. Or they may be way too quiet. Our culture in the United States (and in some other cultures) is grossly undeveloped when it comes to supporting suffering people. We think that if we say the wrong thing, it will injure the suffering person or will make that person remember the loss they have gone through. Know this: we are not inflicting pain by acknowledging someone's loss. It is a gift to show that we know they are suffering. We are not reminding them of a great pain. They don't forget. When we connect with other people's pain, we are sharing the burden. It is compassion. When we avoid other people's pain, is it because we just don't want to feel uncomfortable or burdened ourselves?

Being alone in our suffering multiplies our distress.

Plodding is the same thing as persevering. That's a hard word, *perseverance*. Maybe because it has the word *severe* in it. We don't want to have to persevere. We'd prefer to slide easily through life. But every serious loss or failure or setback or obstacle or betrayal presents us with a challenge. Will we plod ahead or not? Not to move ahead is dangerous. If we remain frozen in our distress or disappointment, we will not find protection but ever-deepening trouble.

A friend described to me the day he was swimming in the ocean and got caught in a riptide, which swept him away from shore. Not being familiar with the ocean, he tried to swim toward the shore, against the strong current, but found he could not make it, though he was strong and fit. He was getting exhausted. He didn't think he would make it. It was only as he moved parallel to the shore, which is what we are supposed to do when caught in a riptide, that he suddenly found himself freed and able to slowly swim back to shore, collapsing in exhaustion.

Perseverance is not a matter of brute strength or force of will. It is to get to a place where we can get through the day and not even worry about the next day, much less the next year. We don't struggle against the riptide. We don't fight against the loss but move parallel to it until we are in a place where we can slowly, methodically, make our way to safety.

Perseverance sounds severe, and *plodding* sounds clunky, but these are, in fact, the normal ways to get through many phases of life in a broken world. All of the great leaders in the history of the world have persevered through some great difficulty. They persevered and they survived, and then they were able to offer something positive.

The word *survive* comes from *vivere*, "to live," and *sur*, "beyond." To survive means to continue to live.

This is what I realized within hours of Eva's death. She had passed from this life. But I had not. I was still alive and would have to figure out how to be alive the next day and the one after that. I had to figure out how to continue to live.

It sounds strange now to say that. But it was real. Continuing to live was not to be assumed. Perhaps one of us would drop to the ground next. Or not know how to go on. Or not want to go on.

People said, "You need to eat something," which irritated me because the idea of putting food in my stomach made me feel ill. There was no room in my gut, only knots. Why should I care about something as inconsequential as food? I wondered whether I would sleep at night. I worried that I might forget to lock the doors in the evening or pay the bills or do enough work to earn my paycheck. Nothing about normal life was to be assumed. Continuing to live meant constant choices and knowing when to stop and collapse for the day.

Everyone who has to survive faces a serious question: Do I want to survive? Do I want to continue to live? The pain is so great, and what if there is more pain to come? We think about what we had hoped life would be—and now would not be. My life's script was now ripped up, and I did not know how to rewrite it.

By God's grace I was able to sleep soundly at night, and it didn't matter if I ate far less for a while, and I didn't spiral down into the darkness of despair that sometimes happens to people on the other side of great loss. (Anyone in grief who does experience significant changes in sleeping or eating or mood needs to take it seriously and seek medical help. There is no shame in doing so, and a grieving person does not need one problem on top of another.)

Slowly, I came to view Eva's own journey in life as plodding. She developed her own ways of making her way through each day, struggling with illness, until the last day, when the struggle was over. And then, no more shame, no more fight. She crossed the finish line.

5

PLACES

$\mathcal{E}$very experience we have involves place. We are spirit, but we are also flesh. We are always located. And so memories will flood our minds when our bodies go to places associated with great joy or great pain.

One day I stood at the end of the sidewalk in front of our house and I suddenly realized that this was the spot where I had my last face-to-face conversation with Eva. It was a stunning realization that took my breath away. My eyes and throat burned in that familiar way when pain comes rushing into my body and then the stream of tears. This was the spot. A place of historic significance in my life. The end of a sidewalk; the last place I looked her in the face and heard her voice.

Almost anything can be a trigger for grief which produces what is sometimes called "sudden temporary upsurges of grief." One day I walked into a sushi restaurant, sat down, and then came the upsurge when I remembered it was her favorite place to eat, and I ducked out the door. Another day I went to the mall to pace off some anxiety, but then, when I saw the Barnes & Noble bookstore at the end of the mall, a pit opened in my stomach as I remembered how Eva loved the couple of years she worked there as a clerk among stacks of books that were her friends. I left the mall and quickly drove away. I was in the produce section of the grocery store and reached for a box of blueberries, thinking, *Eva will really enjoy these, her favorite fruit.* And then I remembered and recoiled, and my throat felt clutched, and I quickly moved to the checkout.

When we retrace our steps to the places associated with the norms of our lives before and have distress, we may have to back away. Later our feelings may change and we can enter places that were too painful at first.

We returned to Door County a month after the funeral, and to the home where she spent her last day. I had to force myself to walk through those rooms and the specific place where she collapsed, because it was either that or give up on ever returning to the old homestead. Would this work out? There was no way to tell. It was one more way to face the reality. I just pushed my feet through the house.

Places are just places, but they can be spatial markers of deep meaning. Every important moment of our lives is attached to some place. But this is fluid. While there may be some excruciating memory we associate with a town, a building, even a room or a doorway, the present-day reality is different from that bad thing that happened before.

The whole matter made me think about a family trip to Pennsylvania when the kids were adolescents and the day we spent at Gettysburg. I loved the history of the Battle of Gettysburg, as did Ingrid, Eva, and Chris (or maybe I just convinced myself they were interested). Oddly, what I remember most is driving around the entire area of the three-day battle, stopping at many places on the battlefields that had been covered in blood and thousands of bodies on July 1-3, 1863, but now were grassy hills and fields where songbirds chirped and summer breezes pushed the grasses back and forth. I pondered a cannon sitting behind a stone fence, looking odd and misplaced. Did the carnage really happen here? In this lovely Pennsylvania field where butterflies and gophers and katydids now dominated the scene?

Life changes. Bad things happen. Then they are done. A place of noise and panic and desperation becomes quiet. Is the quiet the backside of turmoil? Or is it peace? We make decisions about such things.

I chose not to go to the cemetery in Sister Bay in those early months. I knew too many people who talk about going to the cemetery as if they are visiting a loved one—an idea that was repugnant to me. If I believed that our Eva was in that place where cold stones stand in rows among the grass and the stray dogs bark at night and the winter winds whip, I would go crazy. I did spontaneously drive through the cemetery quickly, by myself, one day at dusk, released the sobs fully, and then drove out.

Her physical remains were there, of course. But not her. Not that beautiful young woman. Like Jesus said, "into thy hands I commit my spirit," and then he breathed his last breath, I choose to believe that this is true of her as well.

I said it out loud to myself in those days, again and again: "Eva is not in danger right now." "Eva is not in pain right now." I would say it out loud several times over until the jitteriness in my chest subsided.

I never wrestled with blaming God for this loss. No anger toward God. Maybe it was because I came to believe long before then that the nature of this world and our existence is that it is broken. I had said goodbye to beloved relatives over the years. I officiated funerals over the years for many people—young and old, mothers and fathers and kids, victims of car accidents and cancer and murder and suicide. Disease and separation and painful longing are so hard but not surprising. I was angry, in a free-floating way, but not angry toward God. This was true for Ingrid and Christopher as well. This was not to our credit. It is just how it worked out for us.

Of course, many people do experience anger or frustration or confusion toward God. This is not irreverent. It is not even a problem to be fixed or lack of faith. Traumatic loss blows up everything. It can take a long time for things to settle down.

In the midst of our angst, we just knew how much we needed the mercy of God.

We would not miss Eva so much if it weren't for the fact that we loved her so much, and she, us. Is the joy worth the pain? Yes, of course.

When we go to places where we feel the sting of our losses, we have decisions to make. For one person the right answer may be *I choose not to go there ever again.* Or it may be *This is hard, but I want to get used to this place along with this new reality.* Or it may be *I must reoccupy this place. It is where I belong. It is what I do. I will not allow loss to create more loss.* That's what I am doing when I step up to the podium in church or sit at my keyboard or sit for a quiet evening in our living room. It is what we did when we made her bedroom in Brookfield into a study, though none of us use it much yet.

A couple of days after the burial in Door County, we began the trip home, driving the two hundred miles back to Brookfield. As I drove a few miles past the cemetery, a crushing sorrow and fear suddenly grabbed me as I realized we were leaving the place of her burial behind, and a desperate feeling came over me. *We are leaving her. Abandoning her. I want to go home, but how can we desert her? She should be coming home too. Should we just turn around and go back?* I pulled into a gas station and wept where no one could see me as I pumped gas. I told myself, *She is not here anymore. She has left this world. I believe this. I have to hold onto this.* And then, back to driving.

Over three years the trips to Door County have gotten a little easier each time. But I still have no desire to intentionally go to places I associate with her or to memorialize her. I can now go to the sushi restaurant with a friend. I go to the cemetery in Sister Bay when there is another burial. I can walk into her bedroom and think of its new purpose. But I have no desire to go to the bookstore where she worked or, for that matter, to look through the bins of her books and notebooks. It is hardest to be in places where she was most alive, with her art or literature. No trips to a national park just yet. For now, her artwork is not on our walls. I expect all this will continue to change in the years to come, but these are not matters of obligation. Choice, instead.

Now I wonder, what am I making of all the important places of my own life? Most of the time we are oblivious to the fact that the places we frequent are developing in our minds as markers of the meaning of our lives. We need to invest the most important places in our lives with significance.

Are we making our home as safe and healthy and pleasant as it can be? Is it a place of refuge? Of peace? We built the house when Eva was two years old and Christopher was an infant. They both told us over the years that we were not allowed to ever move, which we took as a sign that they felt secure there. It's hard to know whether holding onto an important place is healthy or restrictive. It's not worth worrying about now.

I walk through the rooms and halls of the church that has been home for me my whole adult life. I was in the middle of numerous building projects over the years, improving and expanding it all. I've spent thousands of work days there over the decades. The original sanctuary, a third the size of our present sanctuary, is where I sat as a college student, and later gave my first sermon at the church when I was twenty-six, and baptized my children, and officiated at many weddings and funerals, and acted in plays. Sometimes when there is a heavy rainstorm during the week I go into that room, dark and empty as it is, and listen to the voice of the rain and let the memories roll though my head. It is so powerful, in a good way, but I cannot sit there for long. Sometimes I sit in the larger newer sanctuary. It is a beautiful room, but an empty, silent shell without the people there. I recall the place filled with thousands of singing voices or being at the podium, a solitary voice, or the sound of the occasional rainstorm pounding the copper roof. I have a relationship with this building, this important place.

When I'm in a place in some part of the world that is filled with pain, I wonder how people get through their days. A slum in Africa, a street where bullet holes mark the sides of buildings, a hospice. Sometimes these are the places that teach us about the possibility of resilience. Like when I saw kids laughing in a dusty field in Ethiopia as they kicked a soccer ball they'd made of old plastic bags.

A week before my mother died, they wheeled her into a new room in the nursing home where they could better care for her as her lungs failed her. She looked around and said to us, calmly, "Final resting place, isn't it?" I was so shocked by the comment, I didn't know what to say. It was true. She accepted it, though in her last days she said the hardest thing I ever heard her say, "I wish I could have stayed longer."

There is a ministry of redemption for places. Or for the people who occupy different places. A friend of ours who is an excellent gardener has come to our home every few months to create a front entryway display of greenery and branches and pots. It beautifies our front door, redeeming the place.

Hospital rooms can be redeemed. One of my pastoral colleagues who has done literally thousands of hospital visits over the years redeems those artificial, sterile places whenever he bounds in for a quick visit and prayer. He's seen it all. He knows God can comfort us in any circumstance. I've received his visits two different times over the years when I was a hospital patient. Presence alters place.

No wonder the biblical writers say, in so many different ways, God is here—wherever *here* happens to be. In the valley of the shadow, or in the wilderness, or in Babylon or

Rome or Jerusalem, or in a war, at a grave. It may not seem like God is in some places. But we call out because we know there is no one who can exclude God and no place or situation that God avoids.

6

TODAY

Clichés are the lazy way of describing life, unless they are utterly true.

"One day at a time." No better way to put it. When we are in the middle of the worst, when we feel like the ground has dropped out beneath our feet, we have to decide how much we can handle. We know we have to face our circumstances, but we just have to do something when it gets unbearable. We have to plod one step at a time, one day at a time, one hour at a time.

Eight weeks in, the harsh reality still seemed hard to believe. So frustrating. So insulting. How could it be?

We continued to live by making a plan each day—not too little, not too much, but we can't really fine-tune life that much. Whatever the plan for the day was, it was likely to change.

Ingrid felt this was the time to do that difficult thing—going through all of Eva's clothes and deciding what to do with them. I so admired Ingrid's courage in this. The scent of Eva's perfume lingered as Ingrid and her sister placed the clothes in bins and bags. That smell was comforting for Ingrid. For me, it put a knife in my heart. The smell was there, suggesting the young woman was there and was just about to come around the corner. But no. Only the lingering scent.

My part was to sort through books and papers, scrapbooks and picture albums. I could not read anything or gaze at pictures. For us, that would be for sometime months or years later. Her books revealed her personality in a fresh way to me—art books, graphic novels, instructional books on drawing and editing, reference books, literature. Such belongings were precious to the person who chose to purchase and own them because they were extensions of her mind and soul. The books were living expressions. She was so alive when she was healthy. But now the books and papers and pictures will be sealed up in bins and will remain shut and stored until we know what we want to do with them. It's been three years now. There is no rush.

Sealing each bin was like closing a small coffin. I should not have left them stacked on the floor of my study where I spent a lot of time each day. Perhaps I subconsciously wanted to keep looking at them, but it just froze me in misery. After a week I stacked them in a small attic crawl space under the eaves. It felt like the burial all over again.

During this time I was conscious that my brain was being rewired around this harsh reality. Bit by bit it adapted. This is the way we are made. It is how we make it through.

Looking into her bedroom was still like looking into a hole. But it is what we had to accept. Faith propped us up. Faith that a good and beautiful life can only be the creation of a good and beautiful God. And the promise of a peaceful destiny. I chose to focus on being grateful for thirty years with this bright light, even with the dimming of her last years.

Why have hope? Because the alternative is unthinkable. But more than that. There are real reasons for hope. Wishful thinking doesn't get us very far.

What is real is today. I could worry a lot about tomorrow. Part of me wanted to work ahead on the grief, get the pain over with on an accelerated schedule, almost like getting school work done ahead of time. But that is foolish and accomplishes nothing. Today has enough ache, along with the goodness. Jesus said that in the sermon on the mount. "Don't worry about tomorrow."

The past is past. The day of Eva's death was done and gone. And the years of ill health before. History is important, but we can only live one day at a time. One hour at a time. That we can bear. Whether it is an hour of peace and joy or distraction, or an hour of tears and moaning.

Still, it is people who are getting us through. God's grace expressed in conversation over a meal or a note, and still—most helpful—anyone who told us simply that they were thinking about us. It is so obvious to me now, after decades of ministry, that the mission of the community of faith is to receive grace and pass it on. No room for bitterness or resentment in any relationship because hardness always repels grace. Physical death is inevitable. Spiritual decay does not need to be.

Of all the lessons we have learned in the past three years, one of the most important is the truth that we have to live in the present. That sounds like a cliché, of course, but it is so utterly, completely true. This was central to our survival.

In the present moment we live with the pain and the anxiety of the loss, but it is in the present moment that we can make choices about what we will do. Any power that we have is present-day power. We move across the ground beneath our feet right where we stand now—right now—not the ground where we were in the past. And who knows what patch of ground we will occupy in the future? We are on paths that twist and turn, rise and fall. There is no telling what obstacles or opportunities may be around the next bend.

When I found myself thinking much about the past, it amplified the pain of loss. There were, of course, the unavoidable flashbacks. My brain keeps popping them into view. The dark room in the emergency room of the hospital, the moments of lostness when leaving an appointment with a doctor, the disheveled bedroom, the casket, the drawings and paintings. I can't stop the pictures and smells and sounds from jumping out at me. The really good memories felt painful as well. A pleasant memory was a reminder that memory making was at an end.

So I decided to be radically oriented to the present. This was a major adjustment. I had taught history in university classes for years and have a reverence for the lessons and wisdom of the past. But in that first year thinking about the past, our family's history only brought distress. As a leader I was accustomed to spending a lot of time thinking about the future—of developing and building and planning. Now the future seemed foreboding, filled with uncertainties because our family's trajectory had taken us to the edge of a cliff.

But the present—I could handle that.

In that first year I knew I needed to mentally pack away the wonderful memories of our thirty years with Eva. Summer family camping trips to national parks, hilarious embarrassing moments, graduations, deep spiritual conversations. I stored such memories for future access. Ingrid was able to get comfort from those memories right then. It was just different for me. Grief is different for every person. Christopher, who lost his sister, best friend, and confidant— an older sibling he so respected and loved—had to put his grief on hold for a long time. He marched bravely through the early days and the funeral and the rearrangement of the house. He touched base with friends. But then he coasted for a year before talking to a close confidant and a counselor and then moving to a new stage. For that first year he avoided saying her name, though I knew that he was not in denial about his loss. He was just doing what he needed to do. I admired his courage.

Ingrid was able to grasp the goodness. She could speak about good memories and liked placing pictures of Eva where she could see them. She loved being a mom and was able to hold onto the love and fun and beauty of the past. I was glad for her.

I suppose that in the years to come it will seem okay to gradually walk the paths of memory. For now, the memories (or at least their physical artifacts) are in bins in an attic crawl space.

When we are surviving we naturally think ahead. But thinking about the future was frightening, even terrifying sometimes. *What will become of our small family? What if someone else gets mortally ill? How will we handle holidays?*

I found myself wondering how we would get through Christmas. How would we handle that gap in reality before us at mealtime or when it was time to sit down to open gifts and there would be no Eva smiling from across the room when she opened a box of her favorite perfume? But then I realized I was torturing myself. Why should I worry about Christmas in July? It was a waste of time and energy. So costly. We'll get to Christmas when it happens. Today is what is real.

Thinking about the future sometimes carried with it feelings of dread. I didn't know how we could go forward. For many months I believed I would never be happy again. That gradually changed. I can now receive happiness even though I know I am a different person and I will never be happy in the way I once was happy. But that's okay. We can't chase happiness. Surviving is not about running after happiness, which teasingly flits back and forth like a butterfly just beyond our reach. We cannot grab happiness or stick it in our head or summon it up in our chest. Peace is possible because real peace can coexist with pain.

What is real is the present moment. What is past is past. What is future is hypothetical. What is real is now. We can figure out ways to get through the now. That is how we are going to survive.

Today is where we live. It is our habitat. The pieces of life that we have to manage are right here, right now.

This, of course, is the genius of one of the most beloved parts of Jesus' teaching:

Do not worry about your life, what you will eat or drink; or about your body, what you will wear. Is not life more than food, and the body more than clothes? Look at the birds of the air; they do not sow or reap or store away in barns, and yet your heavenly Father feeds them. Are you not much more valuable than they? Can any one of you by worrying add a single hour to your life? . . .

But seek first his kingdom and his righteousness, and all these things will be given to you as well. Therefore do not worry about tomorrow, for tomorrow will worry about itself. Each day has enough trouble of its own. (Matthew 6:25-27, 33-34)

Seeking God's kingdom—that prospect opens treasures of comfort. I suppose that is what was happening in me in those early days when the twin truths of the goodness of God and the providence of God were the stripped-down, rock-solid convictions that kept me going. Jesus loosens the anxieties of the future with his simple mandate, "do not worry about tomorrow."

I was able to handle that, as were Ingrid and Christopher. A couple of weeks off work was helpful, but then it was good to ease back into it, if gradually. The necessities of today give us purpose. Just getting up, getting washed and dressed, putting belongings away, taking out the trash, feeding the pets, paying some bills—these things need to be done today, and it will be bad if they are neglected.

In the early months my energy level was diminished. I had maybe 60 percent of my normal energy. On most days I would hit the wall by mid-afternoon. The energy would come back, very gradually, in the two years that followed.

(In our society time off work for bereavement is often woefully inadequate.)

This has not changed: I can handle today. I value today. There will come a time to unpack the mental scrapbooks of wonderful years in the past. I do not know when, but I don't need to know. Planning for the future is now not as anxiety-producing.

Today is where we act, where we make choices. We all have power and influence in this day. No power to change the past and limited power over our destiny. My rudder is in the water beneath my boat. I need a clear head to know when to turn it this way or that. Today is where we can survive and on some days thrive.

7

SEASONS

*F*riends who have moved away from Wisconsin to some place that is sunny and warm twelve months a year, like Arizona or Southern California, will often say that they really miss living where the seasons change. I'm not sure I believe it because they usually say it on a crisp fall day in October or a breezy spring day, not so much in the middle of winter when it's time to go outside and shovel a foot of snow.

There is a reason the Bible and literature and art speak about seasons and life. In some parts of the world there are just the dry season and the rainy season. Elsewhere there is full summer, fall, winter, and spring. Whatever the case, the seasons remind us that life changes, but it also stays the same. Variation and repetition. People are born and people die. These are the least surprising realities of life, and yet newborn babies inspire elation every time and each funeral has its own poignancy and pain.

After three months had passed, we were leaving summer behind and falling toward a somber autumn. What a hard summer it had been. A daily process of pressing ahead, distracting when necessary, letting grief surge like a tidal wave with all the tears and moaning, then distracting again. By the end of that season all the bills were paid and Eva's belongings given away or packed away. We began to look at headstones, but it would still be many more months before we settled on a design. We went through all the wonderful cards and letters people had sent a couple of times.

Anything at that time could trigger another wave of soulful pain. Spotting her picture, finding her handwriting somewhere—her stylish loopy handwriting—perhaps a quote she wrote down or a to-do list or her hopes for the future if she got healthy.

On her bookshelves and desk were all the tools she used in her work as a freelance editor. She had just gotten her business set up, getting jobs with writers and a major publishing house when her health began to deteriorate. Now the abandoned reference books and computer equipment spoke of a career that had barely begun. She would have been really great at it.

We found an outline of a memoir she wanted to write someday—all funny and warm memories of growing up in happy times. Funny and vivid and poignant. How I wish she could have written that with her wry and loving sense of humor. That would not happen, but I was so glad to know that she had joy as she grew up.

And then came that September coolness in the air that signals "back to school." Ingrid and I always enjoyed sending the kids back to school for another year of learning, developing, and preparing for what we hoped would be a full life. But there was no more *back to* anything for Eva. That's that. We could not go back to the warmth and sunshine of July. Fall was upon us. We could not go back to May to try to save her. Fall was upon us. Some maple leaves in Door County were already losing their green for brown and yellow and orange. There was no stopping it because everything that dies falls to the ground. Cold winds were coming. The grass was brown. The geese would start heading south, singing their mournful song. And then the freezing cold. This is the passageway that is autumn.

We all have to watch out for our friends and family who suddenly experience shocking, frightening loss. They are everywhere. And none of us knows exactly, precisely, deeply, how their loss is affecting them. We cannot truly understand. Our job is not to make them feel better—but to be with them. Our mission is not to manufacture faith. Most people do fall back on faith in God. We the bereaved realize that it is better to suffer with God than to suffer alone. We are built up at the same time that we are torn down. We as family and friends cannot fill in the hole our grieving family and friends stare into. And we must avoid at all costs trying to make our grieving friends feel better so *we* are less uncomfortable. Empathy is the generous act of being willing to enter into the suffering of another and to give that gift just for what it is and wherever it may lead.

That first winter was so hard. I did not want to be driven indoors. I did not like thinking of the cemetery with the frozen ground and the snow blowing into drifts. And I did not appreciate, especially that year, the days growing so short. The waning of daylight at 4 p.m. seemed not right. So we made the most of our indoor life. We sought light where it could be found. Still plodding; living in today.

It is good that on December 22 the sun starts to come back. Each successive day is just a minute or two longer, but that is moving in the right direction. That first December a few friends had organized a special worship gathering on the theme of "The Longest Night." A hundred people from different churches gathered on December 21 in the modest sized Lao Christian Church in Brookfield. They were mostly people who had something to mourn or confess in that year and those who wanted to support those who mourned. The hour was rich in readings and prayers and communion. For a night, a community of lament. The hour ended with a proclamation of hope.

Darkness has no substance in and of itself. It is merely the absence of light.

On the next day the daylight would begin to lengthen.

The prophet Malachi said, "The sun of righteousness will rise with healing in its rays" (Malachi 4:2). We need the light. In every dimension. Light as truth. Light as goodness. Light as awareness. Light as knowledge. Light as life. Christ the light.

I know that I understand things now that I did not before the worst happened. I have little interest in things that are superficial or marginal. I do not worry about public opinion. My sense of well-being does not come from getting praise. I don't have anything to prove. I don't want to lose more, but I feel as though we've come through something worse than we could have imagined, and that refocuses our values. Ironically, this feels liberating. To be freed from what is petty and foolishly self-centered.

Once in a while someone asks whether bad things happen in order that other good things can happen. That is a complicated question. We ought to know that it makes no sense thinking that God purposely inflicts people with pain or causes evil to happen so some better altered reality may emerge. On the other hand, most people want to believe that some good things can happen on the other side of loss. This is what we mean when we talk about finding purpose in suffering.

This is why Romans 8:28 is quoted so often: "We know that in all things God works for the good of those who love him, who have been called according to his purpose." The idea is that God is at work in all of our circumstances, in our gains and our losses. Good things can happen after the worst happens. I have no doubt that I became a leader as an adolescent because my father died when I was very young and I had to grow up fast. I've been rushed to the hospital two different times with serious injuries and learned so much about head injuries and ladders and wheelchairs—knowledge I could only have gained through the trials.

So we go through the seasons again and again. Many summers and many falls and winters and springs also. If we are alert, we will get wiser. "Sadder, but wiser," as the aphorism goes. But there is that other saying of a less-desirable outcome: "older, but no wiser." Better days are ahead, but we have to have our wits about us.

I have found the words about the seasons of life in Ecclesiastes to have new poignancy:

There is a time for everything,
and a season for every activity under the heavens:
a time to be born and a time to die,
a time to plant and a time to uproot,
a time to kill and a time to heal,
a time to tear down and a time to build,
a time to weep and a time to laugh,
a time to mourn and a time to dance,
a time to scatter stones and a time to gather them,
a time to embrace and a time to refrain from
  embracing,
a time to search and a time to give up,
a time to keep and a time to throw away,
a time to tear and a time to mend,
a time to be silent and a time to speak,

a time to love and a time to hate,
a time for war and a time for peace.
  (Ecclesiastes 3:1-8)

And then there is this from Ecclesiastes 7:2-4:

It is better to go to a house of mourning
    than to go to a house of feasting,
for death is the destiny of everyone;
    the living should take this to heart.
Frustration is better than laughter,
    because a sad face is good for the heart.
The heart of the wise is in the house of mourning,
    but the heart of fools is in the house of pleasure.

This makes sense. When the worst happens, we go into "a house of mourning." That is where we live for a season. No one can say exactly how long that season is, but that's okay because we know that things will change, and we will move out of that house. It is not our permanent address, though we will have some grief for years or perhaps the rest of our life. And if anyone scolds us for not "getting over it," don't listen to that person.

"A sad face is good for the heart." It is true. Not that sadness is a good thing, but when your heart is sad, it is best for your face to be honest with your heart, thus keeping you

honest with the people in your life. Our faces are our pre-
sentations of ourselves to the world of people around us.
Our faces cry and whisper and shout; they plead and they
query and they gift. Some people see the sad face of
mourners and move in with compassion, *suffering with* the
mourner. This is so right and so good. Others hope the
mourner will smile, even if forced, because it is uncomfortable being around a sad person. This is disrespectful
and selfish.

One winter day I posted on Facebook a photo of myself
in my chef's apron in our kitchen, pointing to a duck I had
roasted to a beautiful crispy golden brown. I was smiling.
This prompted lots of comments from people. About the
duck. More so, about the smile.

8

LOSS

S ometimes people say that their severe loss is like a hole in their hearts. It is so hard to describe that empty space, that tear in the fabric of the universe. When it happens we struggle to adjust to something or someone who is *not* there. We are adjusting to a negative space, which is completely different from adjusting to a new presence in our life, like when we find a new friend or take home a new baby. What is hard to describe is that we are not just sad about missing someone beloved. We are hearing a whistling wind coming from a space that was filled and is now empty.

You see this empty spot when you walk past the bedroom or look at that chair at the dinner table where no one sits now and there is less conversation, or that speed dial list on your cell phone with a name that goes absolutely nowhere. It is challenging enough in life to adjust to someone who has come into your life, more challenging still when it is someone who has disappeared. In that space they used to occupy, now an empty hole, is a loud silence.

Four months after Eva died I was struck by how different each passing phase was. The early days had been so terrifying. I thought back to how it seemed, in those early days, that death was like a grizzly bear that had invaded the camp of our small family and dragged one away, and I lived with excruciating anxiety that this monster could at any moment drag someone else away without notice. I had to force myself to focus intently on the alternative view of death, that it is part of life, that life is a gift no matter how long, and that the providence of God guarantees that God's love is never diminished. I remembered this sense that Eva was falling off a cliff right before my eyes, and my outstretched arm was not long enough to catch her.

But that moment had passed. There was this new reality that could not be denied. It was time to focus on this truth, and I said it over and over out loud: "Right now, Eva is not suffering. Right now, she is not in pain. I don't have to rescue her." I said it to myself, often out loud, over and over. It helped. It helped a lot.

The terror was gone now, but four months into it pain still lurked in any shadowy moment of any day or night. The emptiness of loss is constant. Ingrid and I can rejoice that we had thirty years with Eva, and that is good but it does not fill in the emptiness. No hug, no conversation, not the slightest sound of rustling from her room. Four months in and I was getting used to that. Reality had sunk in. Accepting a harsh reality is better than forgetting the reality. I would rather go through the day with this reality always within my peripheral vision rather than forgetting and in the quiet part of the day having the reality flash back to mind like getting hit in the head from behind.

How we need to understand the people in our lives who have gone through significant loss. One of the most purposeful things any of us can do is to show compassion and to be present with those who have suffered loss. We all have different preferred ways of doing that. Whether we prefer sending a card, or an email, or responding on social media, or having a face-to-face conversation, or picking up the phone, or sending flowers, that's fine. We just need to do *something*. Don't believe that the best thing is to give your friend or loved one space. In our case the cards and conversations were not a burden but a blessing. If we didn't want the contact, we didn't pick up the phone or we waited to open cards for a few days. We went out in public when we were ready. Those who grieve need to be able to call the shots.

We cannot ignore loss, and we must not multiply it. I am running into more and more people who have suffered one loss on top of another—within their families, in their jobs, in their churches. Some losses we cannot prevent. But we should avoid creating more loss.

Over the years I have tried to have empathy for those who suffer loss. After all, that's pretty central to the calling of a pastor. But I realize that we tend to put loss in categories. People whose loved one died of cancer. Or who lost a spouse. Or who lost a child. But there is nothing generic about grief. It is all personal. Even within my family, the loss of Eva is one thing to Ingrid, something else to Christopher as sole sibling, something different to other relatives and friends. I know it is different for me. I loved being the father of a daughter. It was one of the truly great parts of my life. To try to be reliable, to guide, to learn together, to work together, and, so importantly, to protect. It is hard not to feel like an utter failure when I could not protect my kid from disease and death. That sticks with me. All the time. It is an oppressive thought, but not surprising, and necessary to deal with.

There is nothing generic about grief. Somehow we have to have empathy. To try to understand. To put ourselves in the shoes of the mourner. At the same time, to realize that we will never comprehend what this particular loss means to this particular person. It is a kind of "empathy gap." It's no one's fault. It is just inevitable. But knowing we have an empathy gap, we can choose to have compassion that goes as far as our comprehension and then something more.

Along the way, if it is indeed true that faith, hope, and love are the things that remain, then we rehearse what we really believe (faith), trust that things will be okay (hope), and cherish, cherish, cherish (love) those within arm's reach and those who have slipped beyond. Love has no end.

It was still necessary to look straight at the loss or else comfort would be truncated. This is not to say we should obsess about our losses. Focusing only on the loss hour after hour, day after day, is a skewing of reality. The real world includes that loss which is that ugly gaping hole, but it also includes all the things that remain and the people that remain and the qualities that remain like faith, hope, and love. When we obsess about our losses we give them more power than they should have. We are going to have to live in a new reality, which includes the loss but also good meals, normal conversations with people about the normal things of life, good stories in books or movies. Life goes on. If what we enjoyed with Eva was the best of life, then even in her absence we must believe that the essence of life is irrepressible. Even in our loss we have to lean into the good; otherwise, we contradict the good we enjoyed.

I am fortunate to be married to a very wise woman. One day, when Ingrid knew I was in danger of being paralyzed by the loss, she asked me a question she had been asking herself. "Would we rather have had Eva for just thirty years or not to have had Eva at all?" The question was rather stark, but the answer was so obvious. It helped me focus on grace. That grace was the incredible gift we had of raising this kid and then knowing her as the beautiful, inquisitive, substantial adult she became before illness started to diminish her.

A few weeks after our loss I found myself getting caught up in all of life's normal responsibilities and concerns, and forgetting in the middle of the day what had happened to us. Usually, this happened in the early afternoon. Then, when reality hit, when I remembered, the pain was like a knife thrust into my gut. This happened every day. I decided that I needed to keep the loss in a part of my mind, slightly off to the side, in my peripheral vision. This is hard to describe. It was like holding something in your hand, your arm stretched out and to the side. I wanted to remember the loss because then it wouldn't slip into a hidden place and come jumping out at me. I couldn't keep hearing the news in my head as if it were happening again and again.

No wonder grief is draining.

I have known many people over the years who have lost one of their kids. But only after our loss did I know that I had no idea what their pain was like. I was trying to be empathetic. When I did funerals for young people I tried so hard to comprehend their devastation. But I could not fully understand until it happened to us.

That leaves us with a dilemma. When a friend goes through the worst, whatever that is for them, we are never going to be able to fully understand if it is not something we have been through. When a friend is plunged into the worst, we can—and should—try to imagine what it would be like if the same happened to us. But we are just not able to fully comprehend it if we ourselves have not experienced that particular kind of loss.

So what do we do? Obviously, it would be wrong to not even try to empathize. But we know we can't honestly say, "I understand," if we have not walked that same path.

What we can and must do is to spend a little mental and emotional energy to try to comprehend the friend's loss, but then remember that we cannot fully understand, that there is an empathy gap. It is no one's fault. There is no way to close the gap. We have to assume the gap and then try to extend our love out over it.

So we shouldn't say, "I understand," if we have not been through the same thing. We might say, "I have no words" or "I can't imagine" or "I'm so, so sorry" or "I am here. I am thinking of you today." That is honest, and it is helpful.

If we can do that for others, we are not filling the hole but standing around it with them, showing that while *something* or *someone* good is gone, not *everything* is gone.

9

CHERISHING

One day a good friend handed me a piece of paper with a quote from Dietrich Bonhoeffer. I was stunned as I read it. I read it again and again. In one short paragraph Bonhoeffer perfectly captured the paradox we were living: of cherishing and mourning at the same time. (Bonhoeffer wrote this from his prison cell to Renate and Eberhard Bethge on Christmas Eve 1943, fifteen months before his own death by execution just days before the Nazi regime fell.)

There is nothing that can replace the absence of someone dear to us, and one should not even attempt to do so. One must simply hold out and endure it. At first that sounds very hard, but at the same time it is also a great comfort. For to the extent the emptiness truly remains unfilled one remains connected to the other person through it. It is wrong to say that God fills the emptiness. God in no way fills it but much more leaves it precisely unfilled and thus helps us preserve—even in pain—the authentic relationship. Furthermore, the more beautiful and full the remembrances, the more difficult the separation. But gratitude transforms the torment of memory into silent joy. One bears what was lovely in the past not as a thorn but as a precious gift deep within, a hidden treasure of which one can always be certain.[1]

This is what was so striking to me—that the emptiness we are left with actually preserves "the authentic relationship." That doesn't seem to make sense, but it lined up exactly with what I was experiencing.

As we got to the middle of November, five months after Eva passed away, the comforting summer warmness was gone. It was that time of year I have never liked because the trees are stripped bare, the wind has a bite to it, and I know we have months of cold ahead. The cycle of the seasons—cold and warm, dark and light, inside and outside—always makes me think about the inevitability of death and the promise of life. A hard truth and a good truth.

Gradually we were moving past the sense of unreality in which the main daily thought was: *This can't be. This is not real. Let's fix this.*

I was now thinking of Eva in the past tense, which, on the one hand, is easier than feeling like she is just around the corner and about to come bounding into the room, but is also so painful, because I don't want to think of my Eva as receding ever further from us, deeper into the placeholder of someone "I used to know." I know she will never be older than thirty, doing all the things that young adults do. So I must cherish her as a young adult and then work backwards from there.

It had been a while since I spoke out loud, but for the first time in a long while I spoke words out loud in her direction, through tears: "We love you, Eva. Mom and Chris and I love you. We loved you when you were a baby, when you were a little girl, when you were in school, when you were an adult. We love you so much. We love you today. We will always love you." Somehow it seems like that's all that matters. I just needed to voice it. It's all I ever wanted her to know.

It's mysterious, but love is a present reality, even extended to someone no longer here. That's more bearable than thinking about warm memories from the past nicely chronicled in photo albums but somehow trapped there as well. Eva could fill so many scrapbooks (and she did), but she can't be confined to photos and memory books. Viewing love as an ongoing reality keeps the relationship alive. I can't bear the thought that love comes to an end in an ambulance. I repudiate the very idea.

Scripture tells me Eva is not limited to the past tense. That she is alive, though in a realm that is completely beyond my comprehension. I suppose I could try to imagine the happiest of happy days on earth and project out from there, but somehow that seems like a mind game that would fall apart someday and leave me with nothing. So I proceed in simple trust that God is good because there is no other explanation for the good of Eva's life (and all other good). Eva is at peace. The New Testament speaks of sleep and also of being alive at a new level (as in Psalm 90:3-6; John 11:11-15; and 1 Thessalonians 4:13-15). Our mortal minds are not capable of comprehending either of those conceptions, but that is okay. We can believe it.

It is some comfort to proceed with getting some of my books translated and distributed in different parts of the world with "In Memoriam" and Eva's picture on the back page. She was my editor and was going to be my editor in future projects. That won't happen now, but we're using gifts to the memorial fund set up in her name to help others get books that may help them. We sent a thousand books to Haiti in Creole a year after her passing, all with Eva's picture on the last page. We have partnerships to get books translated and printed for Nepal, Pakistan, Iran, Indonesia, Nigeria, Ethiopia, Latin America, Russia, China, and more to come.

It was good to work, as long as I did not use work as a way of avoiding reality. Faith is necessary whether we are at work or at rest. When we go to bed at night and when we slowly come to wakefulness in the morning. When we're alone and when we're with people. When we're in the middle of disappointing circumstances, and when we're enjoying a moment of grace.

I wanted to have the strength to shout out at the top of my lungs: "Where, O death, is your victory? Where, O death, is your sting?" (1 Corinthians 15:55). Some days I could say it out loud; other days, I could only think it.

That November something truly good and beautiful was pressing in on my mind and heart. The mysterious truth that love is a present reality. So much more than affectionate memories. Not a mental scrapbook, because scrapbooks only contain scraps. It is not that we *had* a relationship with

Eva, we *have* one. Love does not come to an end in an emergency room.

No wonder the Bible calls death sleep. When we put our kids to bed and they finally drift off to sleep (neither of our kids ever fell asleep easily), we feel at peace. We can look in on them before we go to bed. The closed eyes and relaxed muscles in their faces, their arms resting at their sides or loosely holding a blanket, their slow and relaxed breathing, let us know that the quietness is such a blessing. The day may have had laughter and crying and talking and shouting, all the minor pleasures and pains of life. But when sleep comes, there is rest.

I will never see "rest in peace" as a cliché again.

In the past few centuries "rest in peace" has become customary on tombstones of Christians. It was first found as an inscription in the Roman catacombs where Christians buried their dead. The prophet Isaiah in the Hebrew Old Testament said,

> Those who walk uprightly
>   enter into peace;
>   they find rest as they lie in death. (Isaiah 57:2)

Numerous biblical writers speak of death as "falling asleep," like Paul, when he writes, "We do not want you to be uninformed about those who sleep in death, so that you do not grieve like the rest of mankind, who have no hope. For we believe that Jesus died and rose again, and so we believe that God will bring with Jesus those who have fallen asleep in him" (1 Thessalonians 4:13-14).

There are, of course, many theological questions about the afterlife. Many would say the concept of soul sleep contradicts the notion of the immediate blessing of coming into the presence of God. (*Sleep* is a biblical description of death whether or not it means "soul sleep.") And in Christian belief, resurrection with a new spiritual body in a recreated heaven and earth is the final hope.

This all goes far beyond human comprehension. Scripture gives us hints about eternal hope but no detailed description because that state exceeds what our minds are able to understand. Our dog gets excited when she sees packed suitcases and we ask her "want to go in the car?" She leaps and runs through the house and bolts out the front door. But it would be pointless to tell her that we are taking a road trip to the mountains and that there would be rivers to jump in, trails to hike, and that the National Park Service comprises hundreds of parks amounting to 84 million acres in a system established by President Wilson in 1916. She can comprehend "want to go in the car?" but not the details of the destination or the way we get there.

I am perfectly content not being able to comprehend eternity.

We can both miss our loved ones terribly and be glad that their suffering is over.

A trajectory of hope says, God "'will wipe every tear from their eyes. There will be no more death' or mourning or crying or pain, for the old order of things has passed away" (Revelation 21:4).

As much as we cherished and still cherish our daughter, the Creator who chose to bring her into this world cherishes her even more than we can. Otherwise, he would not have created her. I can sleep on that.

10

CHRISTMAS

*I*n C. S. Lewis's tale *The Lion, the Witch, and the Wardrobe*, the land of Narnia is under a curse in which it was decreed it would "always be winter, but never Christmas." As we approached the month of December in that first year, I wished it could be just winter and not Christmas at all.

The last thing I wanted was to gaze at an empty space at the dinner table, at the gift-opening, at the Christmas stockings hung on the fireplace mantle.

When we have come through the worst, coming up on that first Christmas and later Christmases holds its own kind of anguish. But there is an opportunity there, too, to be driven to the core of the true meaning of Christmas.

We knew Christmas would be difficult, of course. Thanksgiving started out okay. I spoke at our church's worship service about remembering, and we gathered with friends on Thanksgiving Day as we always do for the meal. But later that day the void of Eva's absence hit me hard. Our house felt so empty without her. I wept and wept. That's when I realized that the cyclical rituals of our lives, like holidays, which we consider "family time," is when we, the bereaved, face the starkness of our losses.

Christmas is difficult, of course, because that is when we typically gather in our family configurations. In my mother's house, where we had Christmas for so many years, we were nurtured by the care with which she decorated. From when I was a child, she set out the same six-inch painted figurines in a wooden manger: Mary, Joseph, Jesus, an angel, a shepherd, and a few animals. I can close my eyes now and see each figure in detail. The tree was always adorned in the same way. The whole extended family sat around the roast beef, mashed potatoes, and huge pot of mushroom gravy on the dinner table. We sat in the same spots every year until my grandfather died and then my grandmother. We all missed them so much when they passed away. Wonderful people. The chairs were rearranged, one generation poignantly giving way to the next. But now the empty chair of our thirty-year-old daughter was a void that was so much worse than empty.

Weeks ahead of time Ingrid and I discussed how we were going to navigate Christmas. Our sentiments were somewhat different from each other. With her Scandinavian flair, Ingrid always loved decorating the house, top to bottom, with greenery and lights and figurines. When Eva was a small girl, Ingrid arranged for the family the ritual of St. Lucia's Day in which the daughter of the house dressed in white, with a wreath of electric candles on her head, delivering freshly cooked sweets to each family member. Eva loved that. It was etched in our memories.

To do Christmas more or less the normal way would have been Ingrid's preference. My instinct was to pretend that Christmas wasn't happening at all. In the end we compromised, keeping things simple. Christmas dinner was nothing fancy. We gave gifts to each other over a period of days rather than the normal sit-down gift exchange around the tree. I put a few floodlights on the front of the house, but nothing more.

We kept things low key. I wanted to get to January as quickly as possible that first year. I wanted each day to be a generic day—whether Tuesday or Friday or Sunday—to have a few tasks to accomplish. I knew I could survive any old day of the week.

So we took it one day at a time until we reached the New Year.

Christmas is always a great opportunity to take in the wonder of God's great love and to contemplate the miracle of God's saving mission in Jesus. That first year I knew December would be unbearable if I dwelt every day on all the Christmas pageants our kids were in or the surprise presents under the tree or the travel to Grandma's house, and all the other sentimental things. Glimpses were okay. Just couldn't live there. Too soon. Too raw. A year later, and then two years later, Christmas would be less difficult.

We can get through grief, but not by trying to turn it into happiness. Grief has to be grief, and moments of happiness break in on their own.

We can't take holiday traditions and fill in the gap of the person who is gone. That would be a mind game that would quickly collapse into something even harder. Going through grief does not mean trying to make yourself happy. I had to learn that being happy was not the most important goal of my life. That I could have a measure of contentment nonetheless. Peace and hope are far better. And ongoing love.

The love does not need to stop. It cannot stop. There is no "love you, too" coming from that empty room. That's the terrible part. But I choose to believe there is a reciprocated love that is silent to my ears but real nonetheless.

We all wonder how that first Christmas will be for the bereaved families we know. From where I sit now, this is what I'd say: continue to have quality interactions with them. Don't analyze them, and don't think you have to maneuver them out of their sadness. Understand. Don't generalize when you talk about how wonderful Christmas is in the twinkly, candy-cane sticky, shiny-gift-wrap kind of happiness. Church leaders: please lead us into an obsession with the miracle of the incarnation. Go deep, please. Take Christmas seriously. Christmas is wonderful because we can focus on the world-shattering event of God become flesh, which gives us hope for the coming day when there will be "'no more death' or mourning or crying or pain." In that I take great comfort. And joy. Happiness deferred.

I always knew that people who recently lost someone very close to them found Christmas difficult to deal with. What I have learned from others who face a sorrowful Christmas is that we have to do what we have to do to get through it. One family I know went to a hotel over Christmas for several years. A mother told me that it was six years before they put up a Christmas tree. For us the challenge was that Ingrid had always taken great joy in decorating the house top to bottom with traditional Swedish Christmas decorations. She did it for the kids. But we knew that all those sights and smells would only draw attention to the fact that Eva wasn't with us. So on that first December Ingrid set out just a few decorations. We did what our instincts told us to do and were glad when we got to January.

The reduction of Christmas did have one positive benefit. It cleared away some of the clutter—flashy and busy and burdensome—so that we could put the focus appropriately on the coming of the Messiah and the promise of salvation. I found myself driven deep into the mystery of the incarnation.

It has all made me wonder about the purpose of all our special days. Birthdays and Christmas and Easter and Thanksgiving—we all have our rituals on those days. Some people make more of special days than other people. Some go through their whole year by running from one marker to the next, while others barely notice those days. A lot of people feel obligated to do certain things or go to certain places or buy gifts or have parties or put lights on the house—but sometimes it is all obligation, little joy.

Our word *holiday* comes, of course, from "holy day" in Old English. Something that is holy is set apart for some special purpose. We may get time off work, opening us to gain something special from the special day.

Things change when we are in a season of survival. We might be more aware of the actual purpose of holy days. We are aware that there is grace in them that goes beyond nostalgia. It's a good thing to think more about the actual event of the birth of Jesus than just the manger scene set out on top of a coffee table. The light of Christmas, which is the light of Christ, makes the most sense when we experience the darkest of darkest nights.

11

RADIANCE

*Y*ou have to turn the pages of the calendar. Whether you walk or plod or slide from one week to the next, one month relentlessly turns over into the next and you come eventually to the birthday of the one you lost.

Eva was born two days after Ingrid's birthday. I had taken Ingrid out for a nice lunch on her birthday. Naturally, we sat there talking about how our lives would be changing very soon. My mind bounced around, fueled by a steady stream of adrenaline, which was both fun and exhausting. We were electrified. Was the house ready? Did we miss anything in our plan to get to the hospital since it wasn't exactly nearby?

Planning didn't matter much since, on the important day, I walked out of the house without the suitcase and took the wrong exit on the freeway.

At lunch Ingrid was feeling kind of queasy. Would our firstborn come on that day? On Ingrid's own birthday?

Just two days later, January 16. That was *The Day*. The most wonderful event of our lives. Pure joy. Cascading love. Deep gratitude. Trepidation with expectation. Two days later I helped Ingrid into the passenger seat of our Honda Civic outside the hospital, and then took that little baby from the nurse and strapped her in the baby seat. As we drove away from the hospital a great weight fell on my shoulders. Now we are responsible—more than we had ever been before in our lives. Would we know what to do now?

At Eva's one-year birthday we had a truly great day. A crazy-goofy-giddy day with more than a dozen friends and family in the house with January howling outside. Excited talk. Pointy hats all around. Aromatic smells of lunch wafting through the house. And in the middle of it all a bald little baby tucked into her high chair, in front of her a small red-velvet cake with butter frosting with a single candle. She blinked and looked around—at the candle, at the cake, at the people. She was alternately delighted and bewildered when a wave of laughter came from a group joking in the next room. Then came the lighting of that one candle. Wide baby eyes. With permission to maul the cake, she slowly grabbed fistfuls of the cake and pushed large pieces into her little mouth, eyes wider yet, amazed by the feel of butter frosting between her fingers as she squeezed them into a fist. The look on her face said, "Mom—you're okay with this? I can really do this?"

Occasionally now, someone will say, because they have heard compelling things about Eva, "I wish I had known her." I always choke up. It honors her and us. And I think, *I do indeed wish there could have been more time for that to happen. Anyone would have loved to have known Eva or call her a friend.*

I could write a book about this kid, this beautiful young woman, and how she affected others. One day after her death one of Eva's peers said, "She was the most radiant person I ever knew." Radiant—so true, so true. Another person said that one day she saw Eva bounding across the room at the home of someone hosting a Bible study to greet her friends with her beaming smile and thought, *I don't know who that is, but I need to find out.*

Only now do I realize how appropriate it was for her to be named Eva Helen ("life" and "light").

Life and light. It is who she was and what she offered to us. She was humble and more self-critical than she should have been. She never presumed anything. She chose to sometimes get clothes at Goodwill and looked spectacular in them. Eva knew the internal is what matters in life.

As I packed her books and notebooks in order to store them, I was reminded of how intensely she pursued truth and beauty. She read literature that was elusive to me, handwrote long lists of quotes, reflected on the meaning of life. The passages of Scripture that made the most impact on her had to do with the mystery and grace of God. But she also wanted to understand philosophies outside of Christianity. She collected graphic novels and aspired to produce one someday. She sketched and painted and wrote. She was thrilled when someone bought one of her prints at her booth at an art show. She looked at the hard realities of life, including mortality, but had an eye for beauty in corners of life that seemed ugly. Her art reflected both realities. That is the truth; that is the gospel. Not naive optimism. Not superficial happy talk. Not rose-colored glasses.

Eva would not let us get away with dishonesty. That helped me as a pastor. No cliché. No spin. No mindless obeisance. She had a nose for arrogance and self-adulation, and she steered away from people like that. The only thing worse than hypocrisy, in her mind, was betrayal.

I knew that Eva was a reliable window for me into her generation. I asked her one day, "What are the main spiritual issues of your generation?" Her answer propelled me into a study of faith and doubt and became a book, *I Want to Believe*.

Eva was just starting her business as a freelance editor. She was my editor, filtering out not just bad grammar but weak ideas as well. She accompanied me on international ministry trips to Belfast and Argentina, which she loved. So when someone asked, the day before the funeral, whether there was a cause for memorial funds to be designated to, it took us just an hour to come up with the idea for an international book initiative in her name. *Life* and *light*. So, Life and Light Books began.

I can't have a conversation with her today, but I can use the echoes of her voice to help people through the written word all around the world.

In the two years after college, Eva saved up for her dream trip across Europe. She and I spent hours researching exactly the right backpack and the best way to pack. When I drove her to O'Hare International Airport in Chicago, she was as excited as I had ever seen her.

In the next couple of months she jumped from Germany to England to France to Turkey to Spain, and more. I set her up with her smartphone so we could video conference, but this was her time and she let us video talk with her just one time. I could tell exactly where she was through the GPS function on her cell phone. She let me do that, probably rolling her eyes about it.

Eva was a wonderful daughter to Ingrid and me, a true friend to her brother, Christopher.

On one terrible day when he was eighteen and Eva was twenty, she almost lost her brother.

The phone rang at about noon. Ingrid and Eva and I happened to be home at the same time. I could tell from Ingrid's "uh huh . . . uh huh" and the blank look on her face that someone on the other end of the phone was giving some grave news. She hung up and calmly said that it was paramedics who had called. Christopher, they said, was in a very serious car accident. He had been thrown from the car he was a passenger in and would shortly be flown to a trauma center in a Flight for Life helicopter. Stunned, we shuffled through our house, gathering a few things, and walked to the car. Five minutes later as we sped down the interstate I-94 toward Milwaukee, we saw out to the left of our car, at low altitude, the distinctive orange and white helicopter we all knew as Flight for Life flying in the same direction we were driving. It was surreal. I remember thinking: *I don't know if my son is in that helicopter or the corpse of my son.*

I said to Ingrid and Eva, "Look." And then that sweet kid said something I will never forget: "If Chris needs me, I'll drop out of college to help take care of him."

Chris survived, but with head trauma and a nonparalyzing spinal cord injury, and there were years ahead of each of us caring for each other in one way or another.

Eva was a wonderful niece and granddaughter. My sister and Ingrid's sister and both our mothers cherished the one girl child in the family.

Eva was a substantial and influential personality to her friends. Her radiance, when it was there, always made a big first impression. I know her absence left a big hole in their lives too.

Even a little light breaks the darkness. And life is not snuffed out even with physical death.

When we remember someone precious to us, we could focus on their shortcomings or on their goodness or a realistic blend of both. Unless we're constructing a fantasy, there is nothing wrong with highlighting the positive. At funerals we tend to do that, not in order merely to make things pleasant or to engage in happy talk, but in order to learn something about what a life can be. And in order to honor.

I'm well aware that I am inclined to remember mostly her positive qualities, but I know she had her quirks and faults and challenges as well. She could be impatient or avoidant or a little too reactive to things. She liked pointing out to me how she was like me in those ways, with a knowing glance and a smile.

A day before the funeral I posted on Facebook a request: "If you knew Eva, maybe you could post something about her so we can all know."

I was blown away by what people wrote. Her friends used words like *intellectually brilliant, amazing artist, fun and exciting, a little wild, intentional, raw, genuine, real,* and *confident in her faith.* One friend wrote, "I will never forget the way that Eva looked at a person when she was talking to them. She was always so engaged, she truly saw people in a way that I know many others didn't take the time to. I felt like she always *saw* me."

Remembrance is power. We need to let our friends know what our good memories are of someone they lost. Better yet, take a risk and say to your bereaved friend, "Tell me about [the person who is gone]." That is something we hardly ever do for each other. It seems intrusive, but it is not.

Under the right circumstances, the bereaved person will take it as a great gift to be able to share with someone else what they cherish. We are telling them that the life of the one who is gone *matters*.

People assume that the sorrow you have for losing your kid is because of what you personally lost. In fact, what I mourn every day is what *many* people lost. I grieve for Eva's friends. I grieve for what she might have been to so many. I grieve for the hole she left behind in the world. Without her radiance, the world is dimmer.

Eva Helen, we love you. By the work and will of God you remain life and light for us. We will do our best to keep our eyes on the truth and to see light wherever it may be found.

12

MYSTERY

Mystery is part of life and part of faith. Not mystery as riddle or puzzle, which suggests someone holding us in ignorance for a while or playing games with us. The other meaning of *mystery* is realities that are so large, so complex, and so high that our limited minds cannot comprehend them. Mystery as ineffability—truths too great to be described in words. (This is one of the ironies of writing—we try to make pathways with words, all the while knowing that if we're doing it right, we'll keep coming to that cloudy cliff edge beyond which words cannot go.)

In some kind of school yearbook, at age nineteen, Eva had responded to the question, "What do you see God in?" Her written answer: "Mystery. My favorite Psalm, 'what is man that you are mindful of him?' That's what I see in God, this mysterious mercy for me."

When we got to the nine-month mark after Eva died, it struck me that this is the length of time we as parents wait as the hidden mystery of development in the womb unfolds before the spectacular moment of birth. But now we were marking nine months of silence and separation. Ingrid and I were married about a decade before Eva was conceived. That made the pregnancy and her arrival a euphoric time in our lives. On the day of her birth I had so much adrenaline and excitement I couldn't think straight. I inadvertently drove way over the speed limit wherever I went, especially on visits to the hospital. The small, pink, pudgy little creature who had come into this gray world inspired in me more awe than I had ever experienced in life. How could I not be crazy in the head?

There is birth and there is rebirth and there is final birth into the arms of God. All of it a mystery. I don't mind not understanding how a human being can be formed in the womb by the knitting of God, and I don't mind not comprehending eternity. Eva always told me she kind of freaked out when thinking about eternity, and I affirmed her honesty. It showed how smart she really was. It is the wisest people whose breath is taken away by the great mysteries of God. It's okay to feel intimidated by mystery at the same time that it rouses you.

Lately, I've been thinking about something I frequently hear from people who have lost their kid. They say, "It is like a part of you dies." I'm finding that is true. But I used to think that referred to the searing pain of this kind of loss or of missing that kid you used to talk to, eat supper with, discuss the issues of life with. But it is harder than that. It is not just that you feel like a part of you dies.

A part of you *has* died.

For almost thirty years there had been two human beings on planet earth who were carrying forward the DNA Ingrid and I imparted. Only two. For all the thousands of people I've had the privilege of influencing through speaking or pastoring or writing, there really were only two human beings who would carry on our name, our history, our intimate family values. There were two people toward whom I felt a commitment surpassing almost all other commitments, with joy.

And then one was gone.

So the question becomes, what do we do with that kind of existential loss? Can we really heal from our life being severed in that way? Does life suddenly become half as valuable or purposeful? I admit that I could easily feel that way. We feel tempted to shift into neutral and coast to the end of our own life. When a younger loved one does their dying, we suddenly feel like our own dying has been shoved higher on our life's agenda. The feeling isn't really morbid. There is a simple logic to it. Our kid went first, and now we realize how dying is part of the inexorable agenda of living.

But it is not right that dying should suppress living. I know that if Eva were here, it would disappoint her to know that we became apathetic or despondent about life. I know it is possible to bear the deep wound of her loss but keep on walking. When someone loses a member of their immediate family, they have lost *someone* extremely important, but they have not lost *everyone*.

All of us need to realize that—married or single, with kids, without kids. Adopted, foster, biological. They say blood is thicker than water. But we all need more moms than our biological mom, more dads than our biological dad, more brothers, more sisters, more friends. Both are true: we must be solidly committed to our families, but our commitments must extend far beyond our families. When our biological family shrinks, it makes us wonder if we have a wider family.

If we can accept mystery, we can find comfort that is larger than our rational assurances. When we face great loss, we need that. We need to give up the need to fully understand. We need the liberty that comes from accepting mystery. If the only way we feel safe is with what we can comprehend, then we will never feel as safe as we might. Mystery moors us to realities that exceed our comprehension. Looking to and respecting the mystery of God is not like standing on a cloud but on bedrock.

How a nineteen-year-old could get that is beyond me. Perhaps a supernatural gift, years before hard times set in.

The book of Job in the Old Testament is hard to read. The story of a man for whom the worst is worse than for anyone I have known, including the loss of *all* his children, his health, his reputation. The story confronts us with all the great questions of suffering and loss. We read along in the book, looking for the answers to those questions. We chafe at the insulting answers Job's friends offer him. God enters the story at the end and offers to Job not answers but himself.

Is that adequate? Well, we can think of it this way: When we face great loss, the worst of the worse, will answers to our questions make us feel better? They will not. Answers will not fill the void. They do not replace the person. The hole in our life is still there. So God gives Job, and us, not an answer to pain but himself. God is indignant about death too. That's why, when Jesus arrived at the tomb of his friend Lazarus, his tears were not whimpering but anger.

Job clung to God. And he survived.

13

BROKEN

$\mathcal{I}$t was the first day of May, eleven months after
Eva collapsed.

Time for some spring cleaning. I was about nine feet high
on an aluminum ladder in our garage, reaching for a bin in
the attic space. I do not remember the moment the ladder
collapsed to the side. I only vaguely remember the fall. But
I vividly remember crashing onto the concrete on my side,
knowing instantly that my body was broken. I was conscious but unable to move. Pain shot up and down one
whole side of my body like electric jolts.

I called out to Ingrid, who was in the house, but I knew she was probably at the other end, so it was not surprising that she did not hear me as I called out again and again. I tried to slide my body, but all my muscles felt frozen. Then I shouted as loudly as I could. Still no answer. Then— figuring I might pass out—I screamed at horror-movie levels. When she ran into the garage, I just said, "Call an ambulance," so regretting that she and Chris needed to witness another medical emergency.

Time stood still until I eventually heard the sirens in the distance, growing closer. Now I was the passenger in the ambulance, glad for the injections they gave me to suppress the stabbing pain.

Broken humerus up near the shoulder. Fractured pelvis. Surgery to repair the arm two weeks later. For the following few weeks I lived in the reclining chair in our living room, minimizing movements in order to avoid stabbing pain. I slipped into a wheelchair when necessary, not able to put weight on the side where my pelvis was broken. When they told me I'd be in the wheelchair for up to three months, I knew that that summer, which I was hoping would be a time of healing from our loss the previous summer, was lost. It would be another season of survival. We had to just accept it.

Once again, people poured out grace on us. Help with rides to the hospital, spring yard work, many meals. We were learning the same lesson from eleven months earlier. What gets us through is knowing that there are people who care. Knowing that we are not alone. And knowing that if we can just be patient, wounds will heal.

I gained a whole new perspective on life viewed from a wheelchair, and I look at people who live in them differently now. When in late summer I was able to come to church and shuffle along, leaning on a walker, people applauded as I moved about. It was embarrassing and revealing at the same time. "Look at you!" people said. I felt like a toddler taking first steps being praised by the grown-ups. Time for a brand-new lesson in humility.

The doctors and physical therapists all told me how much worse it could have been. Hitting my head on concrete from that height could easily have been fatal. Twisting a different way, I could have ended up paralyzed. They were surprised I wasn't more badly injured than I was.

Ever since my father died when I was a young boy, I have known about mortality. The question is: What do we do with this hard truth? Is there a way to live in the face of perishing? The thought that injury or even death can come in the blink of an eye?

This, of course, is the great question of the ages, though we are really good at avoiding it. Whole religions and philosophies have been invented to answer the question.

In the early days after Eva's death, two biblical truths were the solid ground on which I could walk, though my walking was slow and plodding. One was the character of God and the other was the providence of God.

The central truth of Scripture is that there is a Creator God and that God's character is all good and all great. This is what I was taught as a child by my mother and others, and what I came to firmly believe as a teenager. In decades of doing pastoral ministry and teaching theology, I keep coming back to that foundation: God is great and God is good. All the attributes of God can be placed in those two truths. When our daughter died, I knew she had slipped from my embrace, just a week before Fathers' Day, but that she had fallen into the loving arms of her heavenly Father, who actually loves her more than I ever could, though I don't know how that could be. An earthquake hit us, I dropped to the ground, but the ground of the truth of the character of God was firm beneath me. Did the question "How could God allow this?" come rushing to mind? Of course. But it was not the first time in my life I had faced that painful question. It made no sense to pitch our tent in that conundrum.

God is great and God is good. God's greatness is about God's ascendancy over this world, over the universe, over all reality. Greatness is about being eternal, absolutely powerful, all-knowing, and other qualities that we will never fully comprehend. God's goodness, on the other hand, is about relational qualities that we know by revelations such as "God is love" and "God is holy" and "God is right." They also tend to be the qualities imprinted on the spiritual DNA of our lives when we were created. This is how God wants us to be because we were made in the *imago Dei*, the image of God.

The other biblical truth that came rushing into my mind in those early frightening days was the providence of God. Jesus said that God knows the number of hairs on our heads (Luke 12:7), that a sparrow does not fall without God knowing (Matthew 10:29). Psalm 139:16 says that God knows the number of our days and so many other things.

It helped me greatly to trust that my daughter lived the fullness of her life in this world, though it seems foreshortened to us.

The truths about the character of God and the providence of God lessen the anguish but do not take it away. The assurance of heaven gives hope but does not lessen the longing to have one more conversation. Our losses do not make me believe less in God but to call out to God more. It is better to cry out to God than to cry alone.

If you know someone mourning a loss, just come alongside them. They are not looking for answers but love. They want to know they are not alone. God's grace through people can help us while we live in "the house of mourning." We live in that house, in that mourning, while we hang onto the mercy of God.

We all want to believe that when we come face-to-face with severe loss, when we have come into the worst, that things can't get worse than that. Yet every day we remain frail and fallible creatures. One kind of brokenness can be added on top of another. We just never know. Again, thank God for compassionate, understanding people. The friends who drove me to the hospital once a week and visited me only later told me what bad shape I was in. I was scruffy and smelly and pale and slow and didn't know it. I was focused on plodding, and somewhat pleased that each week seemed less difficult than the one before.

I visited my mother in the nursing home one day in my wheelchair, making my way down the hallway in a zigzag trajectory because I could only use one arm to push one wheel and shuffled with my feet. The residents of the facility stared at me, surely thinking I was a new resident. That made me speed up. Mom and I chatted that day, wheelchair facing wheelchair. Knowing how much she always worried about me, I thought she would be freaked out by the condition I was in. But by that time she was already declining rapidly from a lung disease that would take her life just a couple of months later and seemed somewhat unaware of my dilemma. So we just had a normal talk, not too much about my wheelchair or hers or about Eva. We talked about other matters of life, some delightful, others pedestrian. But it was good to visit face-to-face again after a few weeks.

What can you do? Back to that "one day at a time" thing. Plod some more; wait for the healing.

14

SAVING

$\mathcal{A}$nticipation is pleasurable when we are looking forward to something truly good; anticipation is awful when we know we're coming to a mark on the calendar that will inevitably bring pain.

I thought I could distract myself on that day, June 2, one year after Eva suddenly died. Ingrid and Chris and I knew it would not help to recall the hour by hour horror as it unfolded then, but it was hard not to follow the contours of those memories so deeply cut like scratches across my brain. One year earlier that day was marked by the text messages, the frantic phone calls, the ambulance, driving hundreds of miles, the gradual realization of the unthinkable. Every minute seeming like an hour. The darkened and silent emergency room, the calls to loved ones that felt like we were inflicting wounds on them.

It was good we were not alone on that day, and again one year later.

When a loved one or friend is suddenly plunged into a day of shock and panic and death—drop everything if you can in order to extend yourself. Call if you can. Go when it feels right. Send a card or an email. They will signal you if they prefer to delay contact. Pray like you're calling out legions of angels. Without hesitation. Without doubt. Without confusion. Your loved one is feeling like they are falling off a cliff. But with love and support, they will not hit the ground and break, and they will make it to the following day where a whole new reality—jagged and sharp—awaits and a new work begins. You will have a hand in saving, which may be the most important thing you do for a long time to come.

On that day that marked a year, Ingrid was in bed with a migraine. I shuffled through the day stuck in my wheelchair, my arm, postsurgery, limp in a sling. I distracted myself with small home tasks, trying to be anywhere in my mind other than where we had been 365 days earlier. It was not a good day. It was one of those days when we know in our gut that it's okay to look away.

After a night's sleep we came to Day 366, and we began to loop around the sun another time. I was very conscious of this. It felt like a relief to begin another cycle of life at the same time that it felt so, so sad to leave Eva ever further in the past.

We are on this spaceship called Earth, and it keeps rushing through space at sixty-seven thousand miles per hour, and we pass through summer and fall and winter and spring. This is our inexorable path. Life goes on. This is survival in its simplest form. We continue to live. The question is, what decisions will we make about *how* we live? Is it possible that dying promotes better living?

I realize that I have held off until the end, here, to bring up one of the most painful thoughts of that first year—and continuing now. It is a question. But it has no answer. The unanswerable question everyone who experiences significant loss has jumping around in their minds.

What if?

What if we had done something different that would have made Eva well? *What if* we had tried one more specialist, though we had brought her to so many and followed every recommendation? *What if* we had been able to get her through until some new treatment was discovered?

Everyone who goes through traumatic loss will be plagued by the question "What if?" Just last week a friend's nephew was killed by a drunk driver. That family was asking, *What if he had not gone out to the store or if he had left home just ten seconds earlier so that his car would not have been in the spot where the collision happened?*

There is no simple answer to such questions.

What if your loved one had boarded a different plane?

What if you had noticed that family member was thinking of taking his or her life?

What if your kid did not go to that school where the gunman entered?

What if, instead of divorce, years earlier you had called off the wedding even though all the invitations were already printed?

What if you had known that new job had such hidden dangers?

What if you had backed out of the driveway more slowly?

What if you had gone to the doctor at the first signs of pain in your gut before the tumor had a chance to spread?

The question tortures us because in the trickery of our mind we are playing out this scenario—*If I could just wind back the hands of time and do one or two small things differently, this bad thing would not have happened.* It is more than regret or sorrow. It is an irrepressible instinct that says, *Maybe I can still fix this*. That makes no sense, of course, but it is so hard to shut it down.

The only answer to "what if?" is radical acceptance.

In the first few days after she passed away, I talked to several of Eva's doctors. They were intense and wanted to talk diagnostically. I understood why a doctor would want to do that. But I had no such interest. Clinical talk left me in anguish. None of that mattered to me. One diagnosis or another would not alter this largest of realities before us: our daughter was gone, and she was not coming back. So I was done with medical questions. I shut off those conversations. Close the file. Turn away.

For a long time I tried to talk back to that voice that said "what if" with all kinds of answers and rationalizations, but eventually I learned to just turn away and let the question drop to the ground. I chose not to engage in a mental fight I could not win. I counseled others to do the same. This kind of radical acceptance is not fatalism, which is empty and purposeless. It is to choose to live in reality, not letting losses steal the glory and beauty of gains.

Where I found comfort was in the providence of God, the belief that our days are numbered but that God holds us. That and the goodness of God. Sorrow was not evidence of

God's absence but proof that God had brought someone so wonderful into our lives, that there is no explanation for the sorrow if not for the goodness.

Going back to the early days, those were the two pillars that felt solid beneath me: providence and goodness. Add to that the kindness of people, and we had a three-legged stool that would bear our weight.

I have thought so many times over the years about what the apostle Paul said in 1 Corinthians 13, a chapter Ingrid and I had read at our wedding. This chapter about love speaks honestly about all the things (and the people) who change or pass away. But "these three remain," Paul says— "faith, hope, and love."

Faith. As we have been surviving we have held onto faith, but not faith in all the small details. Not all the chapters of the theology books on my bookshelves. The hurricane force wind has stripped away loose and sloppy beliefs and revealed what is at the core of that faith, and it is simply God: good and great, imparting to all of creation features of goodness and beauty and purpose. This has been a good thing—to be forced to the center of faith. To let the marginal drift to the margins. To rebuild on foundations.

Hope. We do hold onto hope. Not wishful thinking but assurances that Eva is okay and we will be okay. Hope as trust that we will make it through this. Early on, thinking about the future was terrifying. After one trip around the sun, coming upon every holiday and birthday and death day—and passing through them—made the next time around the sun a little less frightening. And regarding eternal hope, every last vestige of clichés about heaven was stripped away. I had always rejected the false mental images of eternity as walking in puffy clouds, wearing a white robe, surrounded by empty expanses. What an awful image, where heaven is the negation and loss of everything that we love. It still is a mystery far, far beyond our comprehension, but the new heavens and the new earth must be fuller and brighter and better than our greatest holy pleasures on earth.

Love. No wonder Paul said that the greatest of these three is love. What has gotten us through and is getting us through is the love of God, the love of God through others, and the privilege of loving our daughter. Not just in the past but right here, right now. At the end of that first year I felt a greater obligation than ever before to examine whether I was showing more grace and mercy toward others than before. This will not be automatic for any of us. Traumatic loss can easily turn anyone resentful and bitter. Not just being resentful about one's loss but becoming a bitter personality. Severe loss can also diminish our energy to help others. I know I want to help more than ever, and opportunities abound, but I also know that sometimes I have little left to give. Maybe that will change in the years to come.

I suppose in some ways I became more intolerant of pettiness and self-centeredness and superficiality in others, which was the result of having a clearer vision of what is important in life. But integrity demanded that I be just as self-critical as I was critical of others. Traumatic loss does lead us to self-examination, and we may find it difficult to accept what is revealed. I knew that I now had more compassion in my heart toward people going through traumatic loss. I was told that my public speaking and officiating funerals was different than before. But I do confess that sometimes compassion fatigue came more quickly.

One year was just a start.

EPILOGUE

*H*ealing happens over time. The adage "time heals" is *not* true. The mere passage of time holds no healing power in and of itself. Instead, there are mysterious mechanisms built into our created nature that somehow lessen the bleeding and then close open wounds. Scars remain, for sure. Like the six-inch line in the skin over my shoulder that reminds me every time I look in the mirror that I was broken when I fell off the ladder and then went under the knife and then healed, whenever I walk into Eva's bedroom or see one of her paintings or walk through the doorway where she collapsed, I cringe a bit. But it hurts less than it used to, and it passes more quickly.

"What greater pain is there for mortals than to see their children dead?" the ancient Greek playwright Euripides said.[1] That is stark but true. But add to that the apostle Paul, who said that we grieve, but not without hope (1 Thessalonians 4:13). Grief is not a terminal disease but a passage.

I was shocked by how many of my normal activities in life—simple functions—were disabled in the months following our loss.

Early on a friend suggested I take a long walk in the woods for some fresh air and looked surprised when I said that was something I could not possibly do because it would be frightening. Being out in the wild felt too isolated and thus foreboding. I like taking walks now, though not yet in the wilderness. Courage is coming back.

For about twenty months I could not listen to music. Playing songs in the car or at home opened my heart, and the emotions that surged out were too strong, and it also reminded me of how much music was part of Eva's life. Then one day, suddenly, I could listen to music, just like a switch was flipped. Some months later I was able to take my guitar out of its case and do some strumming, the soft tips of my fingers hurting from not having pressed the strings for a couple of years.

After two years I could get on a plane and go to Haiti to do some teaching, but not before because I could not stand the idea of being away from Ingrid and Chris. Then it was a longer teaching trip to Egypt and after that the Philippines. Slow progress, but with caution.

Healing happens over time.

Surviving is different for all of us, however. For some parents who have lost a child, a two-year window includes only a little healing. For others things go back to "normal" much more quickly. We must not judge each other. There is no right or wrong here. We risk wounding each other terribly if we judge them to be too quick to get over things or to be lingering longer than what we think is necessary. I know war veterans who will tell story after story and others who have never spoken a word about what they experienced in combat and perhaps never will. Everyone's grief is different.

It was so hard watching my mother waste away from her lung disease and eventually die in hospice care, just fourteen months after Eva passed away. Yet because she was eighty-seven years old, it was not traumatic as was Eva's death. I was stunned by how different it was. Maybe it seemed more normal because of her age and because she needed to be liberated from her pain, and because she was so deeply wounded by the death of her only granddaughter. It somehow felt okay that she would make her own exit from this life just a little more than a year later, though we all miss her terribly. Eva and her grandma were like each other in many ways. Radiant. They both brought light into any room they were in. Everyone was delighted to be in their presence. This dimming in our lives is hard. But both of them now have freedom from their pain.

We will all have more than one episode in life that we have to survive. One experience should help us be more prepared for the next. Our expectations in life mature. Somehow we learn to accept the unacceptable.

Researchers have discovered again and again that satisfaction in life is directly related to us having a sense of purpose. Having purpose is a matter of how we act day by day. We don't have to be a nurse or a firefighter or the mayor of a city to have purpose. Every day we can do small things that are purposeful. We fulfill purposes through healthy conversations, through letters or emails that have value, through cooking good meals to nourish others.

Eva wanted to do something purposeful with words for her career. She and I shared a love of words. Before the years of being ill she was trying her hand at freelance editing, starting out by proofreading for a major publishing house. She dreamed of authoring graphic novels in later years. She edited a couple of my books.

So when someone asked me on the day we planned her funeral if we wanted to identify a destination for memorial gifts, we came up with the idea of establishing a memorial fund in her name in order to spread helpful literature in needy parts of the world. She helped edit a book I wrote on understanding the Bible so that became the first project. In the last couple of years the fund has helped us get the book into ten different languages. The day we handed out hundreds of Creole version copies in Haiti, with Eva's picture on the interior page, I knew that something good was unfolding.

Beneath her picture on the inside cover of the book are these words:

Eva Helen Lawrenz (1987–2017) had a passion for truth, literature, and the world. "Eva" means life (Hebrew), and "Helen" means light (Greek). Life and Light Books is an initiative dedicated to her memory and for the purpose of glorifying God through the ministry of the written word.

After her birthday I wrote a collection of fifty prayers for kids, all the while remembering the child's faith that influenced me. Now that book is in multiple languages, and I get photos sent to me of kids proudly holding their very own prayer book in their hands.

At some point almost every day I think about how someone somewhere is reading words that might bring them a little more light or a bit more life. I am glad.

I thought that perhaps I would have no desire to spend time in Door County after all this. There seems to be too many of our clan—Ingrid's family and mine—in Little Sister Cemetery, just up the road from where I am typing right now. But they are not there. Life is in other places. Ingrid and I have our own small place in Door County now, my mother's home. We thought it might be hard being there, but it has not turned out that way. We are making it our own, and I know Mom would like to know we are there. Places must make way for the present, as do we.

I choose to live in today. None of us lives in the past (because that is literally impossible), and the future is entirely hypothetical. When memories are good and wholesome, I'll linger there for a bit, but not if the memory makes me bleed. When I have to plan ahead, I'll sketch out the lines of our possible future. But today I will take some pleasure in finishing this epilogue and then making some breakfast for the family, creating my packing list for Egypt, dropping in on a conference, going out to a movie this evening if I can convince Ingrid or Chris—or maybe the day will unfold differently.

Surviving is more than just making it through. To whatever degree we can dedicate ourselves to purposeful activity each day, there will be more strength in our legs. Living is more than pleasure and certainly more than numbing our pains until we limp toward the end of our own days. We live when we give life.

Cooking a meal gives life. So I decided months ago to get back into cooking—Chinese cuisine especially. Ingrid thinks I sometimes spend more time than is necessary cooking a dinner that has extra flavor and interest. But I like doing it. It is better than merely surviving. Giving a talk or a sermon holds the potential to offer a life-giving insight here and there. Any of us who have gone through great loss have something to offer others. Maybe some good advice or practical help. Mostly understanding. So if you're in a survival time now, look around to see if there are others trying to find life with whom you can connect.

If you have read this book and it has somehow conflicted with your own experience of loss and grief, please do not worry about it. Our family's experience is going to be different from that of others. We are all on the same journey, with different pathways.

There is so much good even though we have to face the bad. Lean into it. Cry out to God. Cling to whatever keeps you going. Cherish those you love. Receive grace when it is extended to you. Offer grace to others.

Life goes on. It's worth it.

Appendix 1

PRACTICAL MATTERS OF GRIEVING

Carry each other's burdens, and in this way you will fulfill the law of Christ. . . . [F]or each one should carry their own load.

Galatians 6:2, 5

Note from the author: Years before our family's loss I cowrote two books on grief and trauma. This appendix, which may contain practical advice that will help, is adapted from Mel Lawrenz and Daniel Green, Life After Grief *(Waukesha, WI: WordWay, 2015).*

Grieving is an inner process, a personal journey. But it can be helped along greatly if the mourner is aware of many practical issues. There are so many questions mourners face: Should I seek out other people? Do I change my work patterns? Should I try to go on as if nothing has happened? Would I be better off if I moved at this time? Should I allow myself to cry? Do I lessen my responsibilities? There are ways mourners can help themselves get through the house of mourning in a constructive, healthy way.

Guarding Your Health

Deep mourning is not only a spiritual and psychological experience, but it affects one's physical life as well. This should come as no surprise since our inner and outer lives are so woven together. A grief response may include reactions of fatigue, confusion, and low energy. When grief is complex or long term and thus complicated, other factors may come into play, like depression.

It is so important for those plunged into grief to keep healthy patterns of eating and sleeping as much as possible. Mourning can cause a person to lose their appetite or develop unusual patterns of overeating as a way of covering over pain. Some variation from usual patterns is to be expected, but long-term undereating or overeating is dangerous.

Sleeping may be affected during mourning. There is nothing unusual about that. But if lack of sleep or effective sleep becomes a long-term problem, then it needs to be dealt with because sleep deprivation becomes a compounding problem. A combination of altered eating and altered sleeping patterns with feelings of hopelessness or despair may point to the onset of depression. A grieving person experiencing those symptoms should not delay in seeking the help of a psychologist, psychiatrist, or physician.

Someone in mourning may not feel like being physically active or exercising, but lethargic behavior over an extended period of time creates its own set of problems. Something as simple as walking can have great benefits to overall physical and mental well-being.

Some people may be tempted to use drugs or alcohol as a way of dulling their sense of mental, emotional, and spiritual anguish. The signs of abuse of substances include drinking alone, recurrent use that interferes with responsibilities at work or at home, continued use in spite of the expressed concern of others, taking risks, and the like. When a mourner realizes they have slipped into such patterns, then they should immediately confide in someone trusted and truthful, and seek professional help, at least on the level of consultation.

Our own physical health can be the furthest thing from our mind in the case of traumatic loss, like the sudden death of a loved one. It seems trivial when other people express concerns regarding eating, sleeping, and social contact. But wise and loving advice needs to be heeded. Mourners need to maintain healthy patterns of mind and body or else the grief can become long term and debilitating.

Sometimes those going through grief feel that there is something wrong in taking care of themselves. There is a sense of shame in going on with life when someone close dies—after all, it could have been you; maybe it should have been you (some people think). The phenomenon known as *survivor guilt* can cause a person to neglect their own well-being. This does not honor the loved one who has passed away.

Lifestyle Issues

When serious loss occurs, there will be a process of adjustment going on inside the mourner, which is grief itself, and those adjustments may very well affect the lifestyle of the mourner in areas like the pace of life, levels of responsibility, and decision making. Expectations are a major issue. When we mourn we may place on ourselves all kinds of expectations, and the people we know will have their own expectations. Some want the mourner to go on as if nothing has happened, perhaps thinking that the best road to healing is to get right back into the prior way of life. But the opposite is possible as well: that others will assume the mourner is some kind of invalid. Neither of these extremes is helpful.

One of the top issues of lifestyle is pace. Mourning may feel like walking through molasses—everything takes longer, seems to require more thought and more effort. Since everything takes longer to do, some people feel ashamed that they are not as valuable or useful as they used to be. This, of course, is a false perception. Grieving does reduce us for a season, but there is nothing wrong with that.

Grief zaps one's energy. Loss is like a serious wound. In today's fast-paced society we sometimes get a certain momentum going that carries us through a rapid-fire string of activities every day. Loss and grief will alter that. Mourning is a time of reflection, and there needs to be time and energy for it.

Then there is the issue of responsibilities. Mourners need to understand, as do people around them, that they may need to ease back into their previous responsibilities. Where it is possible, it is good to return to work gradually. Of course employers have different standards for what they allow (oftentimes standards that profoundly underestimate the effects of loss). While you may get time off of work if you lose a parent, that doesn't mean you will if you lose your best friend, which in some circumstances could be a more grievous loss. A person mourning a traumatic loss should honestly tell their supervisor the circumstances and seek the most humane and sensible path going forward.

People in deep mourning should not feel reticent about seeking the help of friends or family members for housework and maintenance, bill-paying, childcare, and so on. There is nothing shameful about asking for such help. Other people will not automatically step in. The person in grief probably needs to ask for help and to be specific and reasonable.

Sometimes a serious loss requires unexpected decisions. A widow, for instance, may need to decide to get a job (or a different job), learn new skills, perhaps even move to a different house or apartment, or to another state or city. These are major decisions that need to be approached carefully and cautiously. In such circumstances mourners need to actively seek good advice from people who know them well and from legal, medical, or other professionals as need be.

Too much change too quickly is not good. If there is no necessary reason to sell the house, move to a new community, sell the business, get a different car, or something similar, there is reason to hold off on such decisions. Mourners may feel like distancing themselves from the things that remind them of who was lost, but making rapid changes may not reduce pain at all. It can, instead, add loss on top of loss.

Some of the seemingly simplest changes can be the hardest. When, for instance, do you change the room or get rid of the clothes and other personal belongings of someone who has died? Being abrupt is not good, but putting off such adjustments for many months is not good either. Most people will want to keep certain physical objects as mementos to help remember the good parts of the past. That is healthy. Death does not destroy relationship.

It is not uncommon for those who lose a spouse to find a new companion, sometimes quite quickly (this is especially true for widowers). There may be any number of reasons why that new person suddenly steps into the gap, but it should be recognized that widows or widowers cannot take a shortcut around grief by finding a substitute. If a new relationship is wholesome and viable, that's wonderful. But any decision for it to be permanent must be made on objective grounds, not out of a sense of emotional need. There needs to be time. The one-year mourning period of widows or widowers may now be regarded as old-fashioned and artificial, but there is wisdom in customs of the past where it was socially acknowledged that those who grieve do spend time in "the house of mourning."

SUPPORT FROM OTHER PEOPLE

It can hardly be stressed enough how important other people are in the healing process of grief. Sadly, it is also true that other people can add considerable complications to mourning. On balance, however, it is best to look for connections with others. What follows are suggestions for how to find the right kind of support from the right kind of people.

Don't be afraid to ask. If the person in mourning tells others that everything is just fine, then personal support will be stopped before it has begun. People going through grief need to be aware of their own attitudes toward personal needs. Some have grown up in a stoic environment. The way they deal with personal pain is to suck it up and not to show their neediness or vulnerability. Others may be afraid of imposing on other people. They may even have an instinct to take care of other people when they themselves are the ones in obvious need (and, unfortunately, there are other people who will take advantage of that). Yet none of this is a fair and mutual arrangement, and healthy relationships depend on mutuality. If you are willing to help someone else in need, then make sure you allow them the opportunity to help you.

Realize that you may need to express specific and concrete needs. It would be wonderful if those around the grieving person would think carefully and creatively about what they could do to be helpful and then offer it. Some people are insightful and concerned enough to say, "I would like to offer to come and cut the grass on Saturday mornings" or "You pick a day when I can take care of your kids for the whole day so you can go and do whatever you want" or "I'll rearrange my schedule so I could go with you to talk to the funeral director—that is, if you want me to." What is more likely is that well-meaning people will say something generic like, "You just let us know if you need anything." They may feel awkward, not knowing whether it's an imposition to offer anything more, not knowing whether you want someone around or want people to keep their distance.

The grieving person may really need help. Maybe they need assistance with funeral preparations or with taking care of practical things in the days following a funeral. Many people need help with settling an estate or making good decisions because of changes that have been imposed on them. Others need temporary help with home maintenance or meals. There probably are people who are willing to help. What they need is a specific and concrete request.

Mourners may worry about rejection: What if I ask for help and no one is willing? That risk becomes less if we turn to people who we believe have a basic concern for us, and if we bear in mind that when someone cannot come through, it may be circumstantial, and it certainly does not reflect poorly on us.

Keep realistic expectations. When people are deeply grieving they want the pain to go away, the gap to be filled in. Often, mourners will find that time spent with friends and companions can lift their spirits, make them think about other things, but then when they are alone again, they feel the emptiness. They may think that next time they will avoid social contact because it is too painful to feel the letdown. On the whole, however, it is better to have those moments of the fresh air of companionship than not. Over time, it will become easier to sense the benefits of being with other people. It will begin to feel normal again.

One thing that will not be helpful is to expect other people to be able to fill the space left by the loss. To use an analogy, if the family dog is killed by a car in the street, a parent may be tempted to comfort the stunned children by promising to get them another dog, to which they will inevitably react that they don't want a new or different dog—they just want their old friend back. With the passage of time, it just may be that getting a new puppy is healing, but not a substitute for saying goodbye to old Spot.

Mourners may have unrealistic expectations, but it is even more likely that other people will have unreasonable expectations. Well-meaning friends can make the mistake of trying to get a widow or widower into a dating relationship in an untimely or awkward way. They may expect that getting back to work a week or so after the funeral will make all that grief melt away. Expectations during a season of grieving can make the process complicated and difficult. Like a river that cuts its own course, the process of grieving must take place naturally and at its own pace.

Seek people who understand. When we suffer loss, one of the things our hearts long for is someone else who can understand. It's amazing how healing that contact, even in brief conversations or knowing looks, can help the person who is grieving. Not everyone is capable of understanding and empathy. The grieving person may need to actively seek them. They are often found outside the circle of previously known friends and family members. Sometimes it's a pastor or a counselor; other times it's a friend of a friend with whom a simple phone conversation can be reassuring or enlightening.

Support groups can be tremendously helpful in dealing with grief. They are composed of people sharing the same kind of loss, and their agenda is usually very simple: to provide mutual understanding and support. Some may meet for just a few weeks, others are long term. Some are structured; others are simple in format. The hosts may be churches, hospitals, mental health clinics, or others. There are support groups for many situations, including

- new widows or widowers
- parents who lose a child
- children who lose a parent

- parents who have a stillborn child
- people who lose their jobs
- terminally ill people
- people working through the grief of chronic illnesses

It is sometimes difficult for those in grief to have the courage, trust, or energy to seek such resources. Other people can help by making phone calls, getting details, even going with the grieving person to register. Grieving people should tell themselves, however, that there is nothing to lose by trying it, and that multitudes of people would testify that they found more healing by going to a support group than they ever expected to find.

One excellent way to find understanding is to read books written by insightful and compassionate people about the kind of loss you are going through. Granted, it's not the same thing as a warm hug or a face-to-face conversation, but the advantage of seeking such resources is that you will find specific insights to help you cope with and grow through the particular kind of grief you are facing, be it the death of a child, grieving with someone who lost a loved one to suicide, recovering from divorce, or a multitude of other circumstances.

WHEN GRIEF GETS COMPLICATED

Uncomplicated grief is that normal but difficult process of adapting to a change resulting from loss. It is grief the way grief is supposed to work, not easy, not pleasant, but necessary.

Complications can develop, however, that impede the progress of grief. They prevent emotional and situational adjustments, and thus the grieving slows down or even gets stuck. It is when grief becomes delayed, or chronic, or exaggerated. The mourner feels overwhelmed and may behave in ways that only make it harder to get through the grief.

Two of the most common manifestations of *complicated grief* are depression and anxiety.

Depression. Grief itself is not depression. This point is extremely important. Some people think of grief and depression as the same thing because both include sadness and pining, feeling lost and in pain, being less active and less motivated. When a person is grieving, these reactions are normal. (Indeed, their absence is abnormal when serious loss has occurred.) Grief is not a problem to be fixed but a process to be lived out. A mourner may speak in terms of "feeling depressed," meaning a pervasive sense of sadness. Depression in the full or clinical sense, however, goes much further.

Clinical depression is when someone is so overwhelmed that their personal life is disrupted and shows signs such as poor appetite, loss of weight, difficulty in sleeping, a sense of worthlessness or hopelessness or despair, or even suicidal thoughts. Depression is not just having a bad day here and there, but when it seems difficult to survive every day. When people grieve, the world may look harsh and empty, but when they move into depression they look at themselves as part of the bleakness.

The grieving person may focus on the loss that has occurred, but when serious depression sets in there is a more generalized sense of distress. In a similar way the mourner may have a sense of anger toward the cause of the loss, but when a mourner becomes depressed their anger becomes much more diffuse or even directed at the self. A depressed mourner will tend to withdraw from other people rather than accept their offers of comfort or assistance, or may even be irritated or agitated.

Here then are some signs that indicate that grief may have become complicated by serious depression and thus require other forms of assistance:

- physical disturbances such as weight loss or gain, loss or increase of appetite, insomnia
- a sense of despair or hopelessness about life

- a sense of personal worthlessness, shame, or no self-esteem
- an inability to function in normal environments (on the job, at home, etc.) due to excessive crying or pervasive sadness
- suicidal thoughts
- when these signs reoccur some time after the loss occurred
- when these signs become a regular pattern for six months or longer

Because serious depression can be a personally devastating experience, it warrants seeking professional help via the services of a psychologist, psychiatrist, or other competent therapist. The good news is that depression is treatable. Many people have walked through the dark valley of depression stemming from their grief, and with the right spiritual, psychological, and medical assistance, they have come through the other side, though depression can also be cyclical.

Anxiety. With all of the complex things happening during a time of mourning, it may not be noticed that the person has a significant problem with anxiety, which can pave the way for depression. Some anxiety is normal, whereas serious anxiety may be experienced as panic attacks, phobic (fear) reactions, or a general sense of anxiety about everything.

A panic attack is when a person senses a loss of control, great distress, impending doom, and physical arousal (e.g., a racing heart, accelerated breathing, or excessive muscle tension). Phobic reactions are when someone has an unusual fear or avoidance of an object, person, or place. It may be fear of a room in the house, having dinner with the family, or having contact with other people. Anxiety can also come out as obsessions or ruminations.

In any case, here too the mourner needs something more than the passage of time to get past the difficulties. Racing anxiety stands in the way of the internal adjusting process of grief and will only prolong it. Professional help may include the development of skills to bring down the level of anxiety or medical treatment.

Complicated grief needs to be taken seriously. Whether the problem is serious depression, anxiety, or physical disturbances, the mourner does not need one profound problem added on top of another.

Grief may become complicated when a loss in the present is the catalyst for grieving over losses of the past. Unresolved losses can have a cumulative effect. If a person experiences very strong or complicated grief for something that doesn't seem to warrant it, they should investigate whether the present loss is tying into incomplete grief from the past.

Though grief always feels like an unwanted imposition (because none of us wants to lose something or someone important to us), that does not mean that we are helpless. We can help ourselves by linking ourselves to sources of strength and stability outside ourselves. The help is there. We are not alone.

Appendix 2

MATTERS OF FAITH

Note from the author: Years before our family's loss I cowrote two books on grief and trauma. This appendix, which may contain practical advice that will help, is adapted from Mel Lawrenz and Daniel Green, Life After Grief *(Waukesha, WI: WordWay, 2015).*

Serious loss can feel like having something torn from you or like the ground you were standing on is shifting and changing, making you wonder what will come next. What can you count on in life? What is it that won't change? And what can you hold onto now that isn't going to disappear as well?

It is the things that remain that help us get through grief. That includes people who are important in our lives and who are capable of sympathetically standing with us for the long haul. While other people cannot replace our loss, nevertheless, it is a good thing that they are there. They may not know exactly how they can help us in our mourning. They may make mistakes or be insensitive. It's a hard thing to try to understand what someone else is going through. Yet those people who have a genuine concern may be some of the most important resources a mourning person has.

Even more important, God remains. In our experience it may be hard to grasp that fact when someone or something central in our lives is suddenly gone. If the earth suddenly disappeared, the moon's movement would be radically altered; it would even appear to spin out of control, a lost satellite. But the rest of the solar system would still be there; the sun and its massive influence would remain unchanged; its light and heat and energy still available.

Mourners do adjust to their losses and that is why they mourn. The experience of loss makes them look at life from new perspectives. They realize that they had thought of some things as permanent and unchangeable, but then they learned otherwise. For example:

- the wife whose husband only lived a year into the retirement that they had been planning for decades
- the young couple who assumed they could have children whenever they wanted but who faced serious infertility ten years into their marriage

- the fifty-year-old executive who was released from her company and no other company is interested
- the husband who learned of his wife's affair and her almost simultaneous filing for divorce
- the first-time parents who drive home from the hospital alone because their child was stillborn

What do we do when some of our simple and basic assumptions in life are suddenly wrecked?

Because everything in life is subject to change—everything—the Bible talks as frequently as it does about God's unchangeable character.

I the LORD do not change. So you, O descendants of Jacob, are not destroyed. (Malachi 3:6)

The plans of the LORD stand firm forever, the purposes of his heart through all generations. (Psalm 33:11)

You remain the same,
    and your years will never end.
The children of your servants will live in your
        presence;
their descendants will be established before you.
    (Psalm 102:27-28)

The LORD himself goes before you and will be with you; he will never leave you nor forsake you. Do not be afraid; do not be discouraged. (Deuteronomy 31:8)

After talking about the many things in life that are temporary and pass away, the apostle Paul said, "And now these three remain: faith, hope, and love" (1 Corinthians 13:13). If there is anything for us to seek and hold onto when we grieve, it is these three. They are the spiritual moorings that keep us linked to God and grounded on a larger reality when someone or something has disappeared from our lives. They are truths that cannot be contradicted, gifts of God, and characteristics of life that carry us through even traumatic events. They remain, and they help us remain. But how exactly do faith, hope, and love help us to go on?

GRIEF AND FAITH

Faith is belief. It is to hold onto something greater than ourselves. During times of loss it is very important to keep referring back to the developed beliefs that have carried us along in life. Sudden or severe loss may shake our beliefs, or we may discover that there was something important missing from our beliefs. But beyond all that, any faith that we had prior to the loss should be held onto and developed further.

Some people find themselves thrust back onto some of their most basic beliefs, remembering even childhood prayers that comforted then and still comfort now.

Other people find that times of worship have heightened importance. They know that something powerful is going on deep in their minds and hearts, and worship is a time when matters of the soul are respected and cultivated.

It is not unusual, on the other hand, for grieving people to find worship difficult. Sometimes it is because they have a hard time being around other people, but it can also be just because their hearts feel raw—like they've been bruised and cut on the inside. They find themselves reacting to things that are said, feeling easily hurt or agitated. This is not very different from a person who has a broken foot and to whom any bump or pressure can feel excruciating. With time the pain subsides, the injury heals.

Faith means stretching beyond ourselves and getting our life moored to something more stable than ourselves. Nobody is in a safe position being adrift in the currents of life, much more when those currents turn into the violent waves of a storm when serious loss occurs.

For those people whose only mooring was a person they lost, they will face a severe faith crisis. What they believed in was a person. But people change, people leave, people die. It is never too late to find faith in something bigger than another person. People find new faith in God all the time.

The only reason faith can remain is that God remains. Faith in and of itself is the act of believing and trusting. The ropes that moor a boat alongside a secure dock are meaningless in and of themselves unless there is a dock to attach them to. So it is not faith itself that saves—it is God.

Faith is not an elaborate structure that we build with our own insight and ability, a tower reaching to God so we can have access. Quite the contrary, God has come to us in the person of Jesus Christ. Knowing that we are unable to find truth ourselves, God came to teach us. Since we are unable to reform ourselves, God came to change us. And because we are unable to come up with the strength that we need to survive in a loss-filled world, God came to empower us.

For some people and at some times, faith is a strong shout of strong belief; at other times it is just a whisper for help. Either one will do because faith is simply the opening between our needy existence and God's superabundant grace.

Faith is built by listening to the voice of God. That's how all relationships of strong trust are built. The Bible, because it is God's own word, is an expansive conversation between the God of heaven and the people God made to inhabit the earth. In the Scriptures we find every conceivable kind of loss, real stories of real people who suffered such things as

- death and bereavement
- natural catastrophe
- betrayal
- loss of home
- loss of health
- loss of family
- loss of friendship
- loss of innocence
- loss of freedom

The Scriptures describe real human experience. No matter what kind of loss we may experience, we can find the same thing in the Bible. In it we find scores of people who found ways to hold onto God when they went through times of severe loss. We may feel as though we need some guidance on what parts of the Bible to read when we are grieving, but we shouldn't be afraid to do it. The Psalms and the Gospel of John might be good places to read about why we go through what we do, and what God has done to help us.

GRIEF AND HOPE

In that short list from 1 Corinthians 13:13 ("these three remain: faith, hope, and love"), the next is hope. When we have experienced serious loss, looking to the future can be one of the hardest things for us to do. Facing tomorrow or even getting through today can look foreboding, let alone the years that lie ahead.

Yet hope is what allows us to face the future. It is the belief that we will be okay. It doesn't come to us out of thin air, and it is not wishful thinking. Some people tell others who are going through grief that they should just look on the bright side of things, but that is not hope. When people talk about "hoping for the best" it often doesn't get beyond a wish that the next roll of the dice won't be as fateful as the last one. But real hope is based on something real.

If faith in God is what supports us from behind (that is, past experiences that convince us of God's reality and goodness), then hope is what pulls us ahead (that is, into our future).

Grief is a matter of the soul—it touches us as deeply as any other experience. Numerous times in the Psalms the question arises,

> Why, my soul, are you downcast?
>> Why so disturbed within me?

To which the psalmist says:

> Put your hope in God,
>> for I will yet praise him,
>> my Savior and my God. (Psalm 42:5, 11; 43:5)

This kind of dialogue of the self with the self is exactly like the push and pull of grief on the soul—on the one hand, a terrible inner aching and longing; on the other, a desire to survive, to be able to look to tomorrow and not be afraid.

God knows how crippling grief and trauma can be in our experience. God knows that mourners can feel so weak that they don't know how they can go on. And that is why many mourners find extraordinary strength in God. The prophet Isaiah said:

> He gives strength to the weary
>> and increases the power of the weak.
> Even youths grow tired and weary,
>> and young men stumble and fall;
> but those who hope in the LORD
>> will renew their strength.
> They will soar on wings like eagles;

they will run and not grow weary;

they will walk and not be faint. (Isaiah 40:29-31)

"Those who hope in the Lord." What does that mean? It means trusting that if God has done good things in the past, God will do so in the future. It means believing that God does not change. God is really the creator of the future. God is all about new beginnings, and sometimes a new future is molded with the best parts of the past. In other words, God does not demolish the past to begin a new future. Rather, God restores.

There are many ways that happens. In the case of losing someone close to us, the things that we valued in that person remain valuable, and nobody can take those values away from us. So also, the good memories we stored up in the past will go with us into the future. Those memories are more than just stored images or recorded information. They are parts of who we are, what shapes us today, and to that degree those memories are not imaginary. They are living and they are real. In fact, it is not just that the good and substantial parts of the past may carry on in the future, they almost inevitably will.

When we have warm memories of someone we've lost, it takes great effort to suppress them. Some people try to do that as a way of avoiding pain, but it usually fails. We can't evacuate ourselves of memories of the past, and we shouldn't try. That would only add loss on top of loss.

And then there is the kind of hope that goes beyond all others: hope of eternal life. Now, there are those who believe that when people die, they are at the absolute end. Death is irreparable loss, final silence. Most people living in most places at most times have believed otherwise. They have seen the incredible power of God-given life, the way that spiritual life transcends the merely material, and on that basis alone they have concluded that simple physical death couldn't possibly be the end. But there is more. There is the testimony of the authors of Scripture pointing to eternal life beyond the lives we know now.

Heaven is never described in the Bible as people sprouting wings, donning white robes, sitting on clouds as they hear or play an endless strain of harp music (a state of affairs that, to some, seems more torturous than paradisal). No, heaven is not the comprehensive loss of everything we have held near and dear in this life, but the complete fulfillment of it all. Though beyond our comprehension, the new heaven and the new earth the Scriptures point to is the fullest measure of real relationships, real beauty, real goodness. It is so because the departed believer has drawn closer to the Creator of all good things than ever before.

For those who have a loved one die who displayed no apparent faith in God, the funeral can be especially somber. Many mourners who have faith find themselves rehearsing the fact that "the Judge of all the earth [will] do right" (Genesis 18:25), and that as mere mortals we are not in a position to make eternal judgments. It is not possible for the mourner to hold onto the person who has died, but it is entirely possible, and necessary, for the mourner to hold onto God.

It is an extraordinary joy to be able to celebrate the living faith of someone who died in faith. Grief and mourning, tears and sobbing may still be there—these are not the denial of faith. But with faith is an other-worldly hope, a connection with the eternal, a link of future with future— that of the deceased who enjoys an improved existence in the presence of God, and the future of the mourners who know that God will carry them on in life.

And that is the explanation of this statement of the apostle Paul: we "do not grieve like the rest of mankind, who have no hope" (1 Thessalonians 4:13). We will grieve loss (and so did the giants of the faith and even Jesus himself), but it will not be a hopeless kind of grief.

Hope endures. And it helps us endure.

GRIEF AND LOVE

"These three remain: faith, hope, and love. But the greatest of these is love." 1 Corinthians 13 also says, "[Love] always protects, always trusts, always hopes, always perseveres. Love never fails." There are, of course, many empty and half-hearted expressions of love. Sometimes people fall short of the love they claim to offer.

Yet where there is real love, it has incredible enduring power and value, and for that reason it is able to help the mourner get through grief. Love does not dissipate because of distance. It is not shattered because of tension or temporary conflict. It perseveres when there are difficulties.

When loss occurs, love is not ruined. We may lose a loved one but not lose the love. Death cannot bury memories of love. Love is what turns memories from mere mental data into warm, living remembrances. Like faith and hope, love is one of those experiences of life that remains. It is another mooring available when we feel like a storm surge is pressing hard against us. Like faith and hope, the reason love remains is that it is one of the links that we have with God.

Real love is essentially a spiritual resource. It is not borne of human invention and initiative. The Bible teaches that we are capable of love only because it is who God is.

Love comes from God: "Everyone who loves has been born of God and knows God. Whoever does not love does not know God, because God is love. . . . No one has ever seen God; but if we love one another, God lives in us and his love is made complete in us" (1 John 4:7-8, 12).

On the day Moses received a revelation of God on Mt. Sinai, the event revealed the core nature of God as holy love. "The LORD, the LORD, the compassionate and gracious God, slow to anger, abounding in love and faithfulness, maintaining love to thousands, and forgiving wickedness, rebellion and sin" (Exodus 34:6-7).

No wonder real love has such enduring value. It would not be an exaggeration to say that love is who God is; it is why God made us; it is the substance of good human relationships; it is the reason that life is a process of gain as well as loss. If we are made in the image of God, as Genesis says, and if God is love, as Scripture widely attests, then love is one of those qualities overlapping the divine and the human.

If we did not love, we would not hurt when we lose someone close to us. And the opposite is true: if you want to protect yourself from any sense of grieving, if you want to avoid ever having to be a mourner, then don't let yourself love. But if you make that choice, you will cut yourself off from who God is and who humankind is intended to be. You may avoid the sense of loss, but only because you have caused yourself to lose what is most important in life.

How do we find God's help when we grieve? We ask God to show us what it is that remains even in the face of devastating loss. And much does remain. We ask God to strengthen our faith, lengthen our hope, and deepen our love.

When Jesus himself faced the loneliness and desolation of his own imminent death, he asked several of his friends to abide with him, to remain. His words, embellished by a hymn writer, have often been sung as a prayer by people in need asking God to remain:

Abide with me, fast falls the eventide;
The darkness deepens; Lord with me abide!
When other helpers fail and comforts flee,
Help of the helpless, oh, abide with me.[1]

EVA HELEN LAWRENZ (1987–2017) had a passion for truth, literature, and the world. *Eva* means "life" (Hebrew), and *Helen* means "light" (Greek). Life and Light Books (lifeandlightbooks.org) is an initiative dedicated to her memory and for the purpose of glorifying God through the ministry of the written word.

NOTES

4 PLODDING

[1]See John Appleby, *I Can Plod* (n.p.: EP Books, 2008).

9 CHERISHING

[1]Dietrich Bonhoeffer, *Letters and Papers from Prison*, Dietrich Bonhoeffer Works 8 (Minneapolis: Fortress, 2009), 238.

EPILOGUE

[1]Euripides, *The Suppliant Women*, 1122, trans. George Theodoridis, in "Poetry in Translation," 2010, www.poetryintranslation.com/PITBR /Greek/SuppliantWomen.php.

APPENDIX 2: MATTERS OF FAITH

[1]Henry Francis Lyte, "Abide with Me," 1847.

RESOURCES

Books and other resources by Mel Lawrenz: www.wordway.org

Resources about grief: www.wordway.org/grief